A SECRET VICE

J.R.R. Tolkien (1892-1973) was a distinguished academic, though he is best known for writing *The Hobbit*, *The Lord of the Rings* and *The Silmarillion*, plus other stories and essays. His books have been translated into over 80 languages and have sold many millions of copies worldwide.

Dimitra Fimi, PhD is one of the foremost experts on Tolkien and Fantasy Literature. Her published work includes *Tolkien, Race and Cultural History*, which won the Mythopoeic Scholarship Award for Inkling Studies for 2010. She is currently Senior Lecturer in English at Cardiff Metropolitan University.

Andrew Higgins, PhD is a Tolkien scholar who specialises in exploring the role of language invention in fiction. His thesis 'The Genesis of Tolkien's Mythology' explored the interrelated nature of myth and language in Tolkien's earliest work on his Legendarium. He is also Director of Development at Glyndebourne Opera.

A SECRET VICE

TOLKIEN ON INVENTED
LANGUAGES

BY

J.R.R. Tolkien

Edited by Dimitra Fimi &
Andrew Higgins

HarperCollins*Publishers*

HarperCollins*Publishers*
1 London Bridge Street,
London SE1 9GF

HarperCollins*Publishers*
Macken House,
39/40 Mayor Street Upper,
Dublin 1
DO1 C9W8
Ireland

www.tolkien.co.uk
www.tolkienestate.com

This US paperback edition 2023
1

First published by HarperCollins*Publishers* 2016

All texts and materials by
J.R.R. Tolkien © The Tolkien Estate Limited 1983, 2016

Foreword, Introduction, Notes and Coda
© Dimitra Fimi & Andrew Higgins 2016

A CIP catalogue record for this book is
available from the British Library

ISBN 978-0-00-859176-2

Set in OpenType Adobe Garamond Pro

Printed and bound in the USA by Lakeside Book Company

23 24 25 26 27 LBC 5 4 3 2 1

CONTENTS

Appendices

FOREWORD

'A Secret Vice' is widely considered to be the principal exposition of J.R.R. Tolkien's art of inventing languages. In this essay, Tolkien charts his first ventures in language creation during childhood and adolescence through to the development of his first 'artistic' imaginary languages, which later became the heart of his mythology. It includes samples of these languages in the form of poetry and outlines Tolkien's theories on the aims and purposes of composing imaginary languages within a fictional setting. The essay also outlines and interrogates important views and theories about the nature of language itself, and delineates Tolkien's own bold ideas on language as art, as well as language change and language preferences.

This volume makes available for the first time all the drafts of, and attendant notes for, 'A Secret Vice' currently deposited in the Bodleian Library as part of their holdings labelled MS Tolkien 24. In Part I of this 'extended edition' we present Tolkien's lecture, 'A Secret Vice', delivered in 1931, including new sections not printed before. Part II contains a brief essay by J.R.R. Tolkien on Phonetic Symbolism, which appears here for the first time. Part III presents Tolkien's hitherto unpublished notes and drafts associated with both essays. The present edition, therefore, contains significant new material by J.R.R. Tolkien and shows that the previously published text of 'A Secret Vice' that is printed in *The Monsters and the Critics and Other Essays* was the product of an extended series of notes and drafts, including an entire related essay. Published together, the papers provide an expanded view of Tolkien's thoughts and ideas on language invention and related linguistic notions, especially as they pertain to the relationship between language and art. This additional material also places the essay firmly within the intellectual context of the 1920s and 1930s: the tail-end of the *fin de siècle* vogue for international auxiliary languages (languages constructed to aid international communication, such as Esperanto); the empirical research and theoretical work of linguists such as Edward Sapir and Otto Jespersen on sound symbolism; and the Modernist experimentation with language. Tolkien's 'secret vice' of devising imaginary languages (languages invented for works of fiction) enriched the long tradition of fictional languages and fantasy literature, while simultaneously offering a considered and studied response to intellectual trends of the time. This extended edition situates 'A Secret Vice' within its immediate and larger historical, cultural and intellectual context, and provides extensive notes on both essays and the rest of the new material that is presented here for the first time.

For this expanded edition of 'A Secret Vice' we have tried to be faithful to the text while making it as readable as possible, with minimal editorial intrusion. We have adhered to the conventions below:

- Tolkien was not consistent in using single or double quotation marks, and this text reflects his inconsistency
- Words or phrases which defy decipherment are marked as {illeg}
- Words written above other words where neither is cancelled are divided by a slash: /

- Where Tolkien used abbreviations (e.g., 'Gmc', '&c.', 'OE') we have spelled out the words in full ('Germanic', 'etc.', 'Old English')
- We have regularized some punctuation and (when called for) inserted Tolkien's marginal notes in the appropriate places in the main body of the text
- Tolkien occasionally wrote abbreviated thoughts instead of full sentences, and while this has sometimes resulted in a syntactical incoherence, we have preferred to let these stand rather than to intrude editorially
- Curly brackets are used to denote editorial material, while square brackets are Tolkien's own
- A superscript following a word or phrase in Tolkien's text signals that there is an endnote on this material

Verlyn Flieger and Douglas A. Anderson have justly named 'On Fairy-stories' as Tolkien's 'manifesto' on the art of writing fantasy (*TOFS*, p. 9). This volume aims to confirm that 'A Secret Vice' is an equally indispensable manifesto for the parallel (and – for Tolkien – coeval) art of language invention, deserving of its rightful place in the Tolkien canon. 'A Secret Vice' (and Tolkien's language invention itself) has often been neglected by critics. One of the aims of this edition is to re-open the debate on the importance of linguistic invention in Tolkien's mythology and the role of fictional languages in imaginative literature in general. At the same time, the wealth of new material by Tolkien uncovered and presented here affords readers the opportunity to truly appreciate the original ideas on language and art postulated by one of the most innovative academic and creative linguistic minds of the twentieth century.

We are grateful to the Tolkien Estate for entrusting us with this project and for permission to use Tolkien's manuscripts. A special thanks to Cathleen Blackburn of Maier Blackburn for her support. We are indebted to Catherine Parker and Colin Harris at the Bodleian Library for their generous assistance. For access to the Exeter and Pembroke College Archives we thank Penny Baker and Amanda Ingram. Extracts from the minutes of the Johnson Society are reprinted by kind permission of the Master, Fellows and Scholars of Pembroke College, Oxford. Many thanks also to Andrew Honey at the Bodleian and Simon Bailey at the University of Oxford Archives. We are grateful for invaluable help and advice from Douglas Anderson, Mark Atherton, Carmen Casaliggi, Verlyn Flieger, Nelson Goering, Alaric Hall, John Hines, Carl Hostetter, George Kotzoglou, Philip Leube, Carl Phelpstead, John Rateliff, Claire Richards and Patrick Wynne. Our colleagues Kathryn Simpson, Meryl Hopwood, Kate North, and Michelle Deininger were a constant source of support during this project. Thanks also to Chris Smith, editorial director of HarperCollins, for encouragement and advice; and to Charles Noad for his scrupulous editing and eagle eye. For this paperback edition we would also like to thank John Garth, Harm Schelhaas and Arden R. Smith

We would also like to express our thanks and gratitude to all the members of the Elvish Linguistic Fellowship whose diligent and focused academic editing and analysis of Tolkien's linguistic papers have given us and all students and scholars of Tolkien's invented languages an invaluable corpus of work to study and analyse. Many thanks to Christopher Gilson, Patrick Wynne, Bill Welden, Arden R. Smith and Carl F. Hostetter.

Last but not least, we would like to thank our respective husbands, Andrew Davies and David Thompson, for bearing with us during countless late nights and weekends working on this project.

DIMITRA FIMI and ANDREW HIGGINS

INTRODUCTION

Myth-making and Language Invention

J.R.R. Tolkien spent a large portion of his life creating an extended and complex mythology set in a fully fledged secondary world. Many readers know this world and its legends primarily through *The Hobbit* (1937) and *The Lord of the Rings* (1954–5), although Tolkien composed these works by drawing upon a vast backdrop of mythic narratives developed during a span of more than thirty years. An equally significant part of his life was devoted to the creation, development and refining of a series of invented languages, some fully formed, some partially sketched out, and others only mentioned. Many of these languages would become inextricably intertwined with his invented secondary world and its attendant races, cultures and mythology. From his earliest contribution to the code-like *Nevbosh* in 1907, to the last philologically focused work he wrote in 1972 on the name of the Elf Glorfindel shortly before his death, Tolkien never stopped working on the development of what he would characterize as his 'nexus of languages' (*Letters*, p. 143). That Tolkien saw language invention and myth-making as coeval and co-dependent creative acts is evident from several of his letters. For example, he stated that *The*

Lord of the Rings was '*fundamentally linguistic* in inspiration' and, for him at least, 'largely an essay in "linguistic" aesthetic' (*Letters*, pp. 219–20, emphasis in the original). Moreover, he wrote to his son, Christopher, that *The Lord of the Rings* was an attempt to 'create a world in which a form of language agreeable to my personal aesthetic might seem real' (ibid., p. 264). Finally, in a draft of a letter from 1967, Tolkien summed up his language invention:

> It must be emphasized that this process of invention was/is a private enterprise undertaken to give pleasure to myself by giving expression to my personal linguistic 'aesthetic' or taste and its fluctuations. (ibid., p. 380)

Tolkien's linguistic invention was, therefore, a fundamental part of his artistic output, to the extent that later on in life he attributed the existence of his mythology to the desire to give his languages a 'home' and peoples to speak them (ibid., pp. 219, 264–5, 375). As other of Tolkien's writings reveal, what is closer to the truth is that myth-making and linguistic invention began as separate strands of artistic expression in Tolkien's youth, but very soon became indissolubly bound to, and inextricably dependent on, each other (see *Letters*, pp. 144, 345).

In the 1930s, Tolkien composed two essays in which he explored these two key elements of his sub-creative methodology: myth-making and language invention. In 1931, Tolkien delivered a paper for the Johnson Society, Pembroke College, Oxford, entitled 'A Secret Vice'. He unveiled for the first time to a listening public the art which he had both himself encountered, and been involved with, since his earliest childhood: 'the construction of imaginary languages in full or outline for amusement' (see p. 11). He also proposed that: 'the making of language and mythology are related functions', in fact 'coeval and congenital' (see p. 24). Later that same decade, in March 1939, Tolkien was invited to present the Andrew Lang Lecture at the University of Saint Andrews, and delivered a paper titled 'On Fairy-stories', in which – as Anderson and Flieger point out – 'he declared his particular concept of what fantasy is and how it ought to work' (*TOFS*, p. 9). Tolkien's drafts for this lecture reiterate the centrality of myth and language in his legendarium: 'Mythology is language and language is mythology. The mind, and the tongue, and the tale are coeval' (ibid., p. 181).

This interdependence of invented languages and mythological narrative permeates the entire *legendarium* Tolkien would work on for over sixty years. *The History of Middle-earth* series (1983–96) has afforded readers unprecedented access to Tolkien's creative process, from the first versions of the legendarium and related languages in the 1910s and 1920s, to his latest writings of the 1960s and 1970s, which include complex considerations of the interconnection of language and myth such as the masterful 'The Shibboleth of Fëanor' (*Peoples*, pp. 331–66). In addition, specialist publications such as *Parma Eldalamberon* and *Vinyar Tengwar* have made available Tolkien's linguistic documents that were beyond the scope of *The History of Middle-earth* series (see also 'Coda'). These linguistic works often reveal glimpses of stories that were never developed in full, thus once again confirming the 'coeval and congenital' nature of language and myth in Tolkien's legendarium.

'A Secret Vice' is a defining, and rare, exploration by Tolkien of his own practice of language invention, the personal aesthetic it reflected, and its relation to his mythology, which had been evolving for over fifteen years by that time. The text of the lecture itself, and the attendant drafts and notes that this volume brings to light, focuses on some of the key elements that Tolkien thought were crucial in language invention.

Theorizing Language Invention

'A Secret Vice' opens with a preamble, a number of false starts or preludes, before Tolkien comes to his main topic. He begins with mention of a recent Esperanto Congress in Oxford (1930) and offers some evaluative comments on Esperanto as an International Auxiliary Language (IAL). Tolkien recalls a time during World War I while ensconced in a tent, overhearing a 'little man' who was composing a language *sotto voce*, 'in secret'; but that man, Tolkien explains, remained unforthcoming about his task. Tolkien then references a 'nursery' language, *Animalic* (made up from names of animals, birds and fish), that he learnt as a child. He notes that in contrast to Esperanto, which was constructed as a utilitarian means of international communication, both of the other two examples cited associate language invention with pleasure. Following this somewhat prolonged introduction, Tolkien comes to his topic proper, hailing it a 'New Game' or 'New Art': 'the construction of imaginary languages in full or outline for amusement' (see p. 11).

Tolkien continues his lecture focusing on autobiographical examples, reflecting on his own progression from helping create crude childhood languages to the invention of more sophisticated and developed ones. He mentions *Nevbosh* (the 'New Nonsense'), a language that he co-invented with his cousin, Marjorie Incledon, and which was influenced by English, French and Latin. Nevbosh moved away from the simple substitution of Animalic by phonetically distorting words from learnt languages, but it remained ostensibly a code and fairly transparent for speakers of its source languages. But there were exceptions: Tolkien offers the example of a word that was chosen not based on an English, French or Latin prototype, but because its sound seemed to 'fit' its meaning. This element, coupled with the fact that Nevbosh was shared by only two speakers and was not dominated by the need for communication, makes this childhood language an important step towards the imaginary languages of the older Tolkien.

The next example Tolkien mentions in this largely reflective essay is his first ever private language, created for his personal amusement only and not belonging to a community of speakers: *Naffarin*. In this language he was free to express his own taste for sounds and structure and chose Latin and Spanish as inspiration. Tolkien points out that the 'refinement of the word-form' (see p. 17) made this language a superior specimen compared to Nevbosh and he also talks about the gradual development of a personal 'style' and 'mannerisms' in language invention.

From Naffarin onwards Tolkien claims to have aspired to the highest standard of language creation: he attempted to fulfil the 'instinct for "linguistic invention" – the fitting of notion to oral symbol, and *pleasure in contemplating the new relation established*' (see pp. 15–16). At this point in his talk, Tolkien moves away from a reflective-autobiographical style and proceeds to theorize and evaluate the most important elements of his language invention:

    a) the creation of word-forms that sound aesthetically pleasing;
    b) a sense of 'fitness' between symbol (the word-form and its
        sound) and sense (its meaning);
    c) the construction of an elaborate and ingenious grammar;
       and

d) the composition of a fictional historical background for an invented language, including a sense of its (hypothetical) change in time.

Alongside the detailed exploration of each of these elements, Tolkien includes comments on sound symbolism and whether there is such a thing as a personal 'taste' for language sounds; as well as on the interconnectedness of language and mythology. He also offers four poems as samples of those of his invented languages that he considers to have reached a worthy level of refinement and to express his personal 'linguistic aesthetic'. Although he does not name them, Tolkien here gives three poems in *Qenya*, an earlier version of Quenya, and one in *Noldorin*, which was later reconceived as Sindarin.

Tolkien closes his talk with some thoughts on the merits of writing poetry in an invented language as an abstraction of the pleasures of poetic composition, and a comparison of this practice with the pleasure of reading poetry in an ancient language. Tolkien concludes by contemplating the power of language to send the imagination leaping.

The Languages of Middle-earth

Towards the end of 'A Secret Vice', Tolkien somewhat reluctantly moves from theorizing about language invention to unveiling some key examples of his own Qenya and Noldorin, which by that time had become central to his Middle-earth mythology. To illustrate Qenya, Tolkien gives three poems: *Oilima Markirya* ('The Last Ark'), *Nieninqe* and *Earendel* (see pp. 27–31). For Noldorin, Tolkien offers an untitled poem which starts with the line 'Dir avosaith a gwaew hinar' ('Like a

wind dark through gloomy places') (see p. 32) which incorpo-
rates characters from his legendarium as it had developed by
that time, including the evil Orcs, Damrod the Hunter, and
the Elf princess Lúthien Tinúviel. Tolkien states that he con-
siders poetry to be the 'final fruition' of language development
(see p. 26). Therefore, by delivering samples of his poetry in
his talk, Tolkien was not only demonstrating the theories he
outlined, but also showing that these two imaginary languages
had themselves by late 1931 reached an advanced stage in
conception and composition.

The earliest of these imaginary languages, in terms of concep-
tion, is *Qenya*. Tolkien started inventing Qenya in the spring of
1915 through two key linguistic documents: *The Qenya Lexicon*
and *The Qenya Phonology* (published in *PE* 12). In the *Qenya
Lexicon*, Tolkien invented a series of roots by which related
Qenya words could be constructed. In the *Qenya Phonology*, a
dense 28-page philological treatise, Tolkien laid out the basic
phonetic principles of Qenya, including a series of sound combi-
nation rules, which gave Qenya a specific sound aesthetic. As
Tolkien noted on several occasions, this sound aesthetic was
heavily influenced by his early discovery and passion for the
Finnish language (see *Letters*, p. 214). For example, in his devel-
opment of the Qenya vowel, Tolkien focused on the use of open,
long vowels, and his sound combination rules emphasized a sof-
tening of consonant stops; all elements of Finnish phonetics.
The Qenya *Lexicon* and *Phonology* are the foundations from
which Tolkien constructed names for people, places and items
in the early poems of his nascent mythology. The earliest evi-
dence of this work is in the July 1915 poem *The Shores of Faery*,
which Tolkien described as the 'First poem of my mythology'
(*Lost Tales II*, p. 271). This is the earliest known text in which
Tolkien names several places that were emerging in his mythical

geography by constructing invented names attested in the *Qenya Lexicon* and *Qenya Phonology* (e.g. Eldamar, Valinor, Taniquetil). Andrew Higgins (2015) has analysed the words Tolkien constructed from the roots in the *Qenya Lexicon*, and has argued that Tolkien was inventing the words needed to translate some of his own English poetry into Qenya, and to compose poetry in Qenya itself. Tolkien's use of Qenya for original composition is attested in his early 1916 Qenya poem *Narqelion* (pp. 95–6).

After seeing active duty in the First World War, Tolkien revisited the *Qenya Lexicon* by compiling a list of selected Qenya words called *The Poetic and Mythological Words of Eldarissa* (*PE* 12, pp. 29–112) which developed, and to some extent modified, some of his earlier thoughts on Qenya words and their English translations. Qenya was evolving and Tolkien would soon use it extensively in *The Book of Lost Tales*, the earliest prose version of his mythology. He composed prose fragments and various name-lists related to his mythic narratives, while continuing to develop Qenya independently by creating verb conjugations, pronoun charts and noun declensions. While he was a Reader in English Language at the University of Leeds in the early 1920s, Tolkien made his first complete grammar of the Qenya language (published in *PE* 14, pp. 35–59, 71–86). It would be this work on the *Qenya Grammar*, as well as additional lists of invented vocabulary, that Tolkien would draw upon for his creative work in the 1920s, including the composition of the three Qenya poems he included in 'A Secret Vice'.

The second example of an imaginary language that Tolkien gives is *Noldorin*. Noldorin was a later version of a language he had started inventing in 1917–18, originally called *Gnomish*, or *Goldogrin*. Tolkien had invented *Gnomish* as a language related to Qenya but designed to linguistically model what could happen to a language over many years of its speakers wandering and mixing with other peoples. Gnomish was associated with the *Lost Tales* narrative of the exiled Elves, the Gnomes or Noldoli, who left Valinor and wandered in the Great Lands. To phonetically reflect this sense of exile in Gnomish, Tolkien chose to have this language resemble the sounds of Welsh, a language spoken by an exiled people (the Cymry) who had been forced out of their lands by the Anglo-Saxons and made to live as the *wealas* (the Old English word for 'foreigners' and the origin of the name Welsh) in their own lands. Similar to Welsh and other Celtic languages (such as Irish, Manx, Scottish and Cornish), Tolkien invested Gnomish with a system of mutations, or lenitions, that affect words when they come into contact with other words. Indeed, in most cases the system of mutations in Gnomish is almost identical with that of Welsh. In *The Grammar and Lexicon of the Gnomish Tongue* (published in *PE* 11), Tolkien had invented a fairly complete and ingenious grammar for this language and offered a list of words in Gnomish which represented phonetic shifts to distinguish it from Qenya. As with Qenya, most of the evidence for Gnomish is found in the names of people, places and items in *The Book of Lost Tales*. An example of the difference in the phonetic make-up of Gnomish from Qenya can be seen in the name of the chief god of the Valar, whose name and title in Qenya is *Manwë Súlimo* and in Gnomish is *Manweg Famfir*. At roughly the same time of the invention of Gnomish, Tolkien had also gone back to his *Qenya Phonology* and revised sections of it to reflect the idea that both Qenya and Gnomish derived from a common source called Primitive Eldarin (*PE* 12, p. 2), thereby giving both Qenya and Gnomish a more complex sense of historical depth and coherence. Tolkien would summarize this in the new 'Historical Sketch' section, which introduced the revised version of *The Qenya Phonology* (*PE* 12, pp. 1–2).

In the 1920s Tolkien would revise his work on Gnomish, which he would now call *Noldorin* (*PE* 13, pp. 119–32). While he kept the system of mutations and lenitions, one of the chief distinguishing developments from Gnomish to Noldorin was his re-conception of the plural of the noun form. While Gnomish noun plurals were formed by adding endings to the root, Tolkien decided that in Noldorin one of the ways the plural would be formed would be through the morphological device of vowel mutation (ibid., p. 119). Therefore, the plural of the word for mountain ('amon') was formed by a shift in the two vowels of the word to become 'emyn'*. This change in the expression of the plural made Noldorin even more similar to Welsh than Gnomish, as the plural of Welsh nouns often follows the same pattern (e.g. *bachgen* 'boy' becomes *bechgyn* 'boys', *castell* 'castle' becomes *cestyll* 'castles' and *pabell* 'tent' becomes *pebyll* 'tents'). This characteristic would persist into the next conceptual development of Noldorin, now renamed *Sindarin*, and features often in *The Lord of the Rings*, with such place-names as 'Amon Hen' ('Hill of Sight') and 'Emyn Muil' ('the drear hills') (*Fellowship*, p. 393; *Unfinished Tales*, p. 434). In the untitled Noldorin poem Tolkien includes in 'A Secret Vice' this can be seen in his use of the plural form 'yrch' (Orcs) from the singular Noldorin form 'orch' (see p. 32 below and *PE* 13, p. 151). These new morphological developments would inform Tolkien's composition of his *Noldorin Word-Lists* (*PE* 13, pp. 133–56) and the unfinished *Noldorin Dictionary* (ibid., pp. 157–65), from which are derived many of the words in the poem.

---

* In Gnomish, the word for 'mountain' is *orod, ort*, plural *orodin, ortin* (*PE* 11, p. 63).

The different sound aesthetic of Qenya and Noldorin at the time Tolkien delivered 'A Secret Vice' can be appreciated by comparing the opening lines of the Qenya poem 'Nieninqe' and the untitled Noldorin poem Tolkien included in the lecture:

Nieninqe:	Noldorin Poem:
Norolinde pirukendea	Dir avosaith a gwaew hinar
elle tande Nielikkilis,	engluid eryd argenaid,
tanya wende nieninqea	dir Tumledin hin Nebrachar
yari vilya anta miqilis.	Yrch methail maethon magradhaid

For example, many of the words in the Qenya poem tend to end in open vowels (e.g. *Norolinde, pirukendea, nieninqea*); whereas in Noldorin words tend to end in consonants (*hinar, Nebrachar, magradhaid*) giving Noldorin a different sound aesthetic than Qenya.

As mentioned above, Tolkien outlines four key characteristics that imaginary languages should demonstrate and which are reflected in his own Elvish language invention. The first two of these are interdependent and make more sense when discussed together: the creation of word forms that sound aesthetically pleasing, and a sense of fitness between word form and meaning. Given his love and admiration for Finnish, which inspired the sound aesthetic of the Qenya language, it is not surprising that Tolkien mostly associates the Qenya language with his race of Elves. It is the Elves, after all, who represent the highest and purest of his imagined beings, and who are the primary agents of linguistic creativity in Middle-earth (see Fimi 2008 pp. 99–100). As illustrated in the poetic example above, Qenya words and names tend to contain more open vowels reflecting the Finnish sound aesthetic Tolkien admired.

For example, the name for one of the Elvish towns on the 'Lonely Isle' of Tol Eressëa is Alalminórë ('the land of the Elms') and it is formed from a root ALA meaning 'to spread' (*PE* 12, p. 29). The phonetic make-up of Qenya words in his early poem *Narqelion* (pp. 95–6) clearly shows Tolkien utilizing theories of sound symbolism, the notion that the sound of a word 'fits' its meaning (see below, pp. li–lix). For example, in the first line of the poem: 'N · alalmino/eo lalantila ne súme lasser pínear' ('The elm-tree lets fall one by one its small leaves upon the wind'), the repetition of the clusters /al/ and /la/ suggests the use of 'reduplication', a term used in philology of Tolkien's time to describe the phenomenon of repeated and inverted syllables to create a sound aesthetic and semantic effect. Moreover, the sense of leaves falling one by one is expressed with the verb form 'la-lan-til-a', which conveys a sense of downward motion in the phonetic make-up of its syllable pattern. In the *Qenya Lexicon*, there is a specific category of words that have a poetic, almost 'song-like', feel to them, which Tolkien builds from several roots using the multiplicative prefix *li-*, *lin·*. From this prefix he constructs such aesthetically pleasing words as: *lintyulussea* or *lintutyulussea*, 'having many poplars'; *linta(ta)sarind(e)a*, 'with many willows'; *limpa(pa)lassea(a)*, 'much roaring'; *lintuilindórea*, 'when many swallows congregate and sing at dawn' and *lintitinwe*, 'having many stars' (*PE* 12, p. 53). These examples prefigure the same type of polysyllabic poetic words that Tolkien would give to his ancient tree herders, the Ents, in *The Lord of the Rings*, whose word for 'hill' is 'a-lalla-lalla-rumba-kamanda-lindor-burúmë' (*Two Towers*, p. 465). Tolkien's focus on words that have an aesthetically pleasing sound as befitting to their sense would be contrasted with his invention of words that would seek to produce the opposite effect, even without the meaning of the word being known. His use of open vowels to construct the aesthetically pleasing words for the Elves is contrasted in the *Qenya Lexicon* with hard-sounding words having dense consonant clusters used for creatures of evil. For example, *melkaraukir* (*PE* 12, p. 60) is an early form of the name for the Balrog, the monster that Gandalf the Wizard would encounter in *The Lord of the Rings*. Tolkien's use of sound aesthetic to suggest the nature of creatures and things would become a hallmark of his name invention in his Middle-earth mythology. This use of different sounds for cultural contrast can be seen by comparing the first lines of the Elf Queen Galadriel's lament, *Namárië* in *The Lord of the Rings*, with Gandalf's reading of the inscription on the Ring of Power in the Black Speech (a language invented by the Dark Lord Sauron in mockery of the Elvish languages).

> Ai! laurië lantar lassi súrinen,
> yéni únótimë ve rámar aldaron! (*Fellowship*, p. 377)

> Ash nazg durbatulûk, ash nazg gimbatul,
> ash nazg thrakatulûk
> agh burzum-ishi krimpatul. (ibid., p. 254)

Tolkien was not only interested in inventing pleasing sounds and fitting meanings for individual words; he created groups of related words that displayed a shared sound aesthetic and related morphological meaning. An example of this can be seen in the Qenya root MORO, which itself through primary world word-association suggests a feeling of literal or metaphorical 'darkness' (e.g. by evoking words of Indo-European languages such as 'murder', 'murky', 'morte', etc.). Tolkien used this root to construct a series of words directly and indirectly related to concepts of darkness and, by extension, the night and hidden things.

mōri   night

morinda   of the night, nightly

mōriva   nocturnal

morna, morqa   black

moru   hide, conceal

morwa   unclear, secret (*PE* 12, p. 62)

This particular root would persist in his language invention and was used to form the names of two very dark places in *The Lord of the Rings*: Moria ('Black Chasm') and Mordor ('Land of Darkness'). Tolkien was particularly proud of the 'coherence and consistency' of his word and name invention, which he felt was lacking in 'other name-inventors' (*Letters*, p. 26).

A third characteristic of Tolkien's language invention is his construction of elaborate grammars, an element that very few previous inventors of fictional languages engaged with in such detail. The earliest notes and doodles found in Tolkien's undergraduate essay books reveal that he was fascinated with the structure of languages and the development and change of words over time. He would imaginatively reflect this in the make-up of his own phonologies and grammars, which contain dense and intricate philological notes demonstrating the depth of his knowledge. The sheer pleasure (a word he uses several times in 'A Secret Vice') he derived came in the invention of the intricate nature of these grammars and the complex and detailed philological ideas they explored. Tolkien's grammars reflect a similar structure to the historic and comparative grammars he read in his own academic studies, such as C.N.E. Eliot's *A Finnish Grammar* (1890) and Joseph Wright's *A Primer of the Gothic Language* (1892). Arden Smith describes Tolkien's work on his own invented grammars as starting with 'very detailed material on historic phonology, after which he would move on to the morphology section, before the end of which the manuscript would generally degenerate into a mass of incomplete notes in a virtually illegible scrawl' (Smith 2014, p. 204). However, it was through this very work on invented grammars, phonologies and attendant documents that Tolkien expanded his Elvish languages and, given their intertwined nature, developed new elements of his mythology. It has been said that Tolkien developed the narrative of his mythology through successive small changes to his texts rather than large ones (Scull 2000). Given the evidence of much of Tolkien's early Elvish language invention, it would seem the same was true here; a process of constant 'niggling'.

A good example of Tolkien's linguistic niggling and changing ideas about grammar can be seen in his work on inventing and refining the pronominal system of Qenya, and its later revision in *The Lord of the Rings* as Quenya, the language of the High-elves (see *Return*, p. 1127). In its earliest phase of development (c.1917–18), Qenya pronouns were conceived as immediately preceding a verb and joined by a hyphen. Therefore, 'I come' would be expressed as 'ni·tule' (*PE* 14, pp. 52–3). In an example from a form of Qenya Tolkien used in his 'Father Christmas letter' of 1929, called *Arktik*, this hyphenated form had, by now, split from the verb and become a separate element: 'ni vela' 'I see' (*Father Christmas*, p. 30). By the early 1930s, however, Tolkien started to change his mind once more, and in a document known as *Qenya Conjugations* (*PE* 16, pp. 116–28) he started to express pronouns using suffixes added to the end of the verb form. Tolkien would continue to develop this idea in the Quenya of *The Lord of the Rings*. For example, the penultimate line in Galadriel's lament, *Namárië*, is 'Nai *hiruvalyë* Valimar' 'Maybe *thou shalt find* Valimar' (*Fellowship*, p. 378, emphasis added), where the form -*lyë* ('thou') is added to the end of the verb form *hiruva* ('shalt find'). Given the several detailed notes Tolkien made on this specific passage in the *Namárië* poem, it is clear that by the time he wrote this section of *The Lord of the Rings* he firmly believed that the Quenya pronoun should now be a suffix added to the verb form and only be used as a standalone word form for purposes of emphasis (see example in *PE* 17, pp. 75–6). These series of changes represent a complete re-conception of the placement of the pronoun in the earliest version of Qenya.

The fourth characteristic of Tolkien's language invention is his intertwining of myth and language to create 'an illusion of historicity' (*Letters*, p. 143) through which he could imaginatively reflect how languages change over (hypothetical) time and through the cross-migration of peoples. Tolkien's thoughts here were evidently influenced by two key elements. First, the fact that languages do not exist in a void, but belong to their speakers, who share many cultural characteristics which feed into the uses, conventions and historical developments of language. Therefore, if Tolkien was to achieve progression from the simpler childhood concept of inventing languages for social interaction, to more private and artistic linguistic inventions, then he would need to invent those peoples, cultures and attendant mythologies that would allow these languages to develop and prosper. Secondly, as Tom Shippey has shown, the linguistic paradigm that Tolkien adhered to both as student and as teacher was comparative philology: a discipline which came out of Germany in the nineteenth century and was based on the idea that languages change over time, not randomly, but through the operation of regular sound shifts (Shippey 2005, pp. 32–4). As Tolkien's language invention skills grew, his own invention moved from the creation of isolated, static languages, devoid of historical context or internal development, to families of related languages, each designed to appear to have under-gone characteristic internal development and all emerging from a common ancient source language through long years of grad-ual and systematic changes of sound over time.

Tolkien's narrative of the Elves clearly reflects, and mythically re-imagines, the paradigm that eighteenth- and nineteenth-century philologists explored of the existence of a 'proto-language' spoken by a hypothetical common people, the Indo-Europeans, which through time and migration had become splintered into different language groups and dialects. In Tolkien's basic story, which he developed and refined throughout the evolution of his legendarium, the Elves awake in the East and are invited by the Valar to journey to the West. Some groups of Elves decide to accept this invitation and take part in a great march to the West, while others stay in the Great Lands. This first division is followed by a splintering of their languages. Some of the Elves who march to the West relinquish the journey along the way and form their own social and linguistic commu-nities, while others make the entire journey to the home of the Valar in the West. In a later part of the history of the Elves, a group who come to the West, the Noldoli, are determined to return to the Great Lands and, in so doing, also develop another form of Elvish. In each step of this process of migration and diffusion, different versions of Elvish languages and related dialects are created, whilst these groups also come into contact with other peoples, such as Men and Dwarves, whose own lan-guages are in turn influenced by their contact with the Elves. In c.1937, Tolkien would use the model of the 'Proto-Indo-European' tree of languages to create his own 'Tree of Tongues', which explored how the (now eleven) Elvish languages related to each other as well as to the languages of other peoples in Middle-earth (*Lost Road*, pp. 196–7; see also *PE* 18, pp. 28–9). It would be this expansion of his 'nexus' of languages for Middle-earth that Tolkien would take with him into his writing of *The Lord of the Rings*, and into the work he did on his mythology after its release in his attempt to prepare the 'Silmarillion' for publication. Tolkien's work on establishing both the history and the interconnections of his invented languages would inform his use of these languages in *The Lord of the Rings* and would be the source for the paratextual information Tolkien would give readers in Appendices E and F, which focus on the languages. Tolkien's constant 'niggling' and re-conception of his languages can be further seen in the major change he made in the early 1950s, while working on these appendices. He re-conceived Noldorin, together with its attendant history, redeveloping it into the language that is known by readers of *The Lord of the Rings* as Sindarin (see *Peoples*, pp. 61–2). With the publication of his seminal work, Tolkien's own language invention would not only continue as a private pleasure but would gradually fascinate his readers, many of whom would write to the author eager for more information about his now not-so-private language invention (see also 'Coda').

'A Secret Vice' was, therefore, an important linguistic exposition that allowed Tolkien to reflect on his own language invention thus far, as well as develop his theoretical ideas on imaginary languages. The positive reception of his Elvish languages (albeit by a small audience; see pp. xxxii-xxxiii below) and the self-reflection that writing this paper afforded him may have also encouraged Tolkien to continue practising and perfecting his 'secret vice'. The period immediately following the delivery of the lecture represents the next major phase in the development of the Elvish languages that would first appear in *The Lord of the Rings*. In this phase, Tolkien not only continued to consolidate, develop and refine the two major Elvish languages, Qenya and Noldorin, but also, in line with his developing mythic narrative of the Elves, expand his nexus of Elvish languages to include other variant dialects (some only sketched in a few words or names, and others merely mentioned).

Firstly, Tolkien developed other elements of Qenya, such as the c.1936 'Bodleian Declensions', which added five fully declined noun classes to Qenya (*VT* 28, pp. 9–30). Other examples of Qenya would appear in the untitled song of Fíriel from Tolkien's time-travel story, *The Lost Road* (*Lost Road*, p. 72). A little later, Tolkien also composed the 'Koivienéni Manuscript', two Qenya prose sentences, one concerning the awakening of the Elves and the other the planting of the Two Trees of Valinor (*VT* 14, pp. 5–20). An inscription in Noldorin would also appear on an early version of Thror's map in *The Hobbit* (*Artist*, p. 92).

Secondly, in c.1937 Tolkien wrote *The Lhammas* (Noldorin for 'Account of the Tongues'), in which he sketched out a narrative and internal history of the descent of all the Elvish tongues from (at this conceptual stage) the language of the Valar, the Gods of his invented mythology (*Lost Road*, pp. 166–98). Along with this work Tolkien also visually outlined the aforementioned 'Tree of Tongues', which demonstrated how each of his imaginary languages related to each other and to languages of other races, such as Men and Dwarves (ibid., pp. 196–7). Tolkien's 'Tree of Tongues' was clearly reproducing the Indo-European genealogical tree model (see Fimi 2008, pp. 101–2) and put into practice the idea that imaginary languages should have a 'pseudo-historical background' (p. 25). Tolkien's work during this period culminated in *The Etymologies*, a document from c.1937–8, which revisited his earliest concept of developing words from roots. It presented a series of Eldarin roots, out of which he constructed related words in the twelve Elvish languages or dialects he had devised: Danian, Doriathrin, Eldarin, Exilic Noldorin, Ilkorin, Lindarin, Noldorin, Old Noldorin, Ossiriandeb, Qenya, Primitive Quendian and Telerin (*Lost Road*, pp. 347–400).

'A Secret Vice' and its Immediate Context

'A Secret Vice' was first published by Christopher Tolkien in *The Monsters and the Critics and Other Essays* (*Monsters*, pp. 198–223), alongside six other essays by his father. Christopher notes that the paper:

> exists in a single manuscript without date or indication of the occasion of its delivery; but ... the Esperanto Congress in Oxford*, referred to at the beginning of the essay as having taken place 'a year or more ago', was held in July 1930. Thus the date can be fixed as 1931. (*Monsters*, p. 3)

The 'Secret Vice' papers include other indications of an early 1930s date. For example, in the same folder there is a standard printed postcard from the Curators of the Examination Schools at Oxford, relating to the use of lecture rooms and dated Saturday 7th June (MS Tolkien 24, folio 53v), which indicates that the year is 1930 (Trinity Term). Also included is a list of marks for students at the University of Reading (MS Tolkien 24, folio 47r), some of whom graduated in 1932 and 1933 (University of Reading, 1973; Tolkien served as an external examiner for the University of Reading). A more secure *terminus a quo* can be

---

* 22nd Annual World Congress of Esperanto held in Oxford from 2–9 August 1930.

found in the 'Essay on Phonetic Symbolism', in which Tolkien mentions Sir Richard Paget and his work on sound symbolism (see pp. 68, 83). Tolkien can only be referring to one of two of Paget's books that explore this subject, and both were published in 1930: *Human Speech: Some Observations, Experiments, and Conclusions as to the Nature, Origin, Purpose and Possible Improvement of Human Speech*; or *Babel, or The Past, Present, and Future of Human Speech*.

Further research at a number of Oxford University archives has disclosed that Tolkien indeed delivered 'A Secret Vice' in 1931, as Christopher Tolkien had hypothesized. The minutes of the Johnson Society at Pembroke College reveal that Tolkien read 'A Secret Vice' to the Society on 29th November 1931, at 9pm. The Society was founded in 1871 in memory of Samuel Johnson (1709–1784), author and lexicographer. Although originally a literary society, by the early twentieth century it had become 'practically the J.C.R.* meeting for an (alleged) literary purpose' (Pembroke College Archives Catalogue). Indeed, the contemporary records (1927 and 1932) of the Johnson Society at the time Tolkien delivered 'A Secret Vice' show that topics were wide and varied, including early modern literature, as well as contemporary British, European and American writers.

Tolkien's association with the Johnson Society goes beyond the delivery of 'A Secret Vice'. Tolkien became a Fellow of Pembroke College as part of his role as Rawlinson and Bosworth

---

* 'Junior Common Room', a term taken to refer to the community of undergraduates in any given Oxford College, which is usually run by a President and a Committee elected by students. The J.C.R. is responsible for students' lives beyond their academic programmes (e.g. by organizing social and cultural activities). Each College also has an M.C.R. (Middle Common Room) to represent postgraduate students, and a Senior Common Room (S.C.R.) for academics and other members of staff.

Professor of Anglo-Saxon, to which he was appointed in 1925. The Society attempted on more than one occasion to invite Tolkien as a guest to one of their formal dinners in the late 1920s. In the minutes for 19 June 1927, it is recorded that Messrs R.G. Collingwood and John Masefield were unable to attend the Society dinner, and therefore 'it was decided that the following two gentlemen be invited, Messrs. Ralph Straus and J.R. Tolkien [*sic*]' (Johnson Society Minute Book, PMB/R/6/1/6 1927–9). In the event, neither attended the Dinner, which was held on 23 June. The following year, the minutes of 13 May 1928 show that both R.G. Collingwood and Tolkien were suggested as guests for the dinner of 20 June, but 'the society voted in favour of Mr. Collingwood' (Collingwood by that time had given two papers to the society on Jane Austen, both of which were greeted with enthusiastic reports in the minutes). However, Collingwood was unable to attend and Tolkien was duly invited instead. According to the minutes: 'the society listened to various speeches, which, with the exception of that of Professor Tolkien, were remarkable for their singular lack of wit. Professor Tolkien then entertained the society with a series of amusing stories' (Johnson Society Minute Book, PMB/R/6/1/6 1927–9).

The minutes for the meeting of 29th November 1931 record that:

In Public Business Professor Tolkien read one of the most ingenious papers that the Society has ever heard. The "Secret Vice", which gave the paper its title, turned out to be the study & invention of obscure living languages, or codes. After a peculiar conversational opening, in which he touched on such elementary new languages as those produced by adaptation of already-existing languages, – he cited an example one in which the names of animals were used to denote certain words or phrases, & a whole new language built up on this principle, – Professor Tolkien went on to discuss those languages which were composed of words entirely their own, whether derived phonetically, or from some other (probably dead) language. The most interesting example of the phonetic type of language is that spoken in the island of Fonway, which apparently has no connection whatever with any other known language, nor is it spoken or understood elsewhere than in this one small island. Professor Tolkien finally regaled the Society with works of his own, written in an original phonetic language. He had, he said, on one occasion been surprised & rather dismayed to overhear two navvies conversing in a language which till then he had believed understood only by himself, its originator. The works which he now read, however, he believed to be entirely his own & to be unknown to anyone else.

After a discussion started by the President, in which the conversation drifted down such byways of language study as are formed by the eccentricities of James Joyce & Gertrude Stein, the meeting was declared informal, but continued until after midnight.

(Johnson Society Minute Book, PMB/R/6/1/7 1919–37)

Remarkably, the minutes record the name of only one invented language, but not one associated with Tolkien's legendarium, and which was also omitted from the first publication of 'A Secret Vice' in *The Monsters and the Critics and Other Essays*. What is also intriguing is that the discussion that followed Tolkien's paper made mention of James Joyce and Gertrude Stein, both of whom are referenced in Tolkien's accompanying notes (see pp. 91, 100).

In his edition of 'A Secret Vice' Christopher Tolkien speculates on a possible second delivery of this paper:

The manuscript was later hurriedly revised here and there, apparently for a second delivery of the paper long after – the words 'more than 20 years' were changed to 'almost 40 years'. (*Monsters*, p. 3)

The manuscript does indeed contain a number of emendations, but many of them seem to be contemporary with the first delivery (see pp. 43, 44, 45). There are however three pieces of internal evidence that point to a possible second delivery, approximately 15–20 years from the first one: in addition to the emendation mentioned by Christopher Tolkien in the quotation above, Tolkien changed the words 'this society' to 'this or any other society of philologists' and the words 'for a literary society' to 'for a learned society' (see pp. 11, 12). Bearing in mind that the Johnson Society was – at least nominally – a literary society, it is possible that 'A Secret Vice' was delivered again to a Society with a philological agenda, c.1945–50. The date is intriguing, as during 1945–6 Tolkien was in the process of composing *The Notion Club Papers* (*Sauron Defeated*, pp. 145–327), a novel that was left unfinished, but which explores fascinating ideas on language and myth (see Fimi 2008, pp. 82–3). This novel also introduced a new invented language, *Adûnaic*. However, we have not been able to locate any concrete evidence for a second delivery of the paper. It may be that Tolkien prepared it – or began preparing it – but this second delivery did not happen. If it did occur, it may be that a record exists which will be located in the future. However, it is worth noting that Tolkien became relatively well-known after the publication of *The Hobbit*. It would, therefore, be curious that a second delivery has not been recorded in any of the Oxford periodicals.

The Tolkien who first delivered 'A Secret Vice' on 29 November 1931 was a man actively engaged in social, academic and creative interests, all of which very much informed each other. In terms of his academic career, Tolkien had been Rawlinson and Bosworth Professor of Anglo-Saxon at Pembroke College for a little over five years. During this time, he had a full schedule of teaching, tutorials, attending faculty meetings, supervising students' theses, and, to make some additional money, external examining. Since arriving from Leeds, he had been developing a growing body of his own academic work and research. While at the University of Leeds, Tolkien had co-edited a new edition of *Sir Gawain & the Green Knight* with his colleague E.V. Gordon (1925). Between 1924 and 1927 Tolkien had been a regular reviewer of philological books and publications ('Philology: General Works') in *The Year's Work in English Studies*. In 1925, he published several articles in *The Review of English Studies*, including 'Some Contributions to Middle-English Lexicography' and 'The Devil's Coach-Horses', both of which explored various philological cruxes of Old and Middle English. For example, in 'The Devil's Coach-Horses' Tolkien argued that a specific early English word 'eaueres' is not, in fact, a survival of the Old-English word 'eofor' (boar) but a word that had developed in early Middle English, 'aver', which can be translated as '"property, estate" but also "a cart-horse"' (Solopova 2014, p. 232). Also in 1925, Tolkien contributed a translation to Rhys Robert's article 'Gerald of Wales and the Survival of Welsh' in which he offered a reconstructed version of Geoffrey of Monmouth's prophecy on the survival of the Welsh language using a late twelfth-century version of South Midlands English (see Anderson 2005, pp. 230–4). In 1928, Tolkien published a six-page 'Foreword' to Walter Edward Haigh's *A New Glossary of the Dialect of the Huddersfield District*, a dialect that preserved evidence of influence from the Norse invasions in the eighth and ninth centuries on English word-forms (see Croft 2007, pp. 184–8). In 1929, Tolkien published his landmark analysis, 'Ancrene Wisse and Hali Meiðhad', in Essays and Studies by Members of the English Association. In this highly detailed article, he demonstrated that two groups of disparate devotional works from the West Midlands of the twelfth century shared close similarities in phonology, grammar and spelling. Tolkien coined the term 'AB language' (bringing together labels used to designate the two groups of manuscripts) to suggest that, when taken together, these documents reflected the preservation of a local English scribal tradition, descended from late literary Old English, and which still persisted in the late twelfth century (see ESMEA and AW). On 16 May 1931, Tolkien delivered a paper to the Philological Society in Oxford on Chaucer's use of Northern dialects in 'The Reeve's Tale' of The Canterbury Tales. Tolkien described Chaucer's representation of Northern English dialect in the speech of the scheming clerks of 'The Reeve's Tale' as Chaucer's 'linguistic joke' (Reeve's Tale, p. 2). A characteristic that much of the above academic work shares is a focus on the uses and intricacies of language. In all his academic exploration, Tolkien employed the philological or comparative method to uncover, reconstruct and fill in the gaps in the meanings of lost words, names and their attendant stories.

Another aspect of academic endeavour with which Tolkien was actively engaged at this time was his work to reform the Oxford English School syllabus, in particular the reunification of the teaching of philology ('lang') with literature ('lit'). In his application for the position of Rawlinson and Bosworth Professor of Anglo-Saxon at Pembroke College, Tolkien wrote that one of his aims would be 'to advance . . . the growing neighbourliness of linguistic and literary studies, which can never be enemies except by misunderstanding or without loss to both' (*Letters*, p. 13), and when he took the Chair at Pembroke he duly sought to achieve his aim. In an essay published in *The Oxford Magazine* for 29 May 1930, Tolkien called for a reform of the syllabus that would put a stop to the artificial separation of the study of language from literature and called for the study of philology which combined both areas and which 'is essential to the critical apparatus of student and scholar' (*Oxford Magazine*, p. 778). Shortly thereafter, in 1931, Tolkien's reformed syllabus was accepted and would remain in place for many years. His commitment to the harmonious co-existence of 'lit' and 'lang' evokes his dictum about the 'coeval and congenital' nature of mythology and language in his creative writing.

J.R.R. Tolkien had, by this time, found a great friend and ally in his pursuit of syllabus reform, in the Fellow and Tutor in English Language and Literature at Magdalen College, Clive Staples (C.S.) Lewis. Tolkien first met Lewis at an English Faculty meeting at Merton College on 11 May 1926. Lewis would record his first impressions of Tolkien in his diary: 'a smooth, pale, fluent little chap . . . No harm in him: only needs a smack or so' (cited in *Biography*, p. 143). Initially, Lewis, being in the 'literature' camp, was not a great supporter of Tolkien's proposed 'lit and 'lang' reforms. However, by 1927, Tolkien had got Lewis involved in his newly formed informal club to read Old Norse sagas in the original, 'The Coalbiters' (from the Old Norse *kolbítar*, meaning those who stay so close to the fire in the winter that they virtually bite the coal), and they became great friends and supporters of each other's academic and, to greater and lesser extents, creative work. Lewis would also introduce Tolkien to his colleague Owen Barfield (1898–1997), whose theories on the original unity of language and myth, expressed in such works as his *Poetic Diction: A*

Study in Meaning (1928), would be a considerable influence on Tolkien's thoughts about language (see below, pp. lvii–lix). In the early 1930s Lewis, Barfield and Tolkien would be joined by other colleagues to form a new informal literary club, the Inklings, which has been celebrated as one of the most important literary groups of the twentieth century (see Carpenter 1978; Glyer 2007).

Although Tolkien had a busy academic schedule this did not preclude him from progressing creatively. In addition to exploring projects in both prose and poetry, he was developing new versions of his expanding mythology that intertwined neatly with his language invention. From the summer of 1925 to c.1931 Tolkien revisited his earliest version of the tale of Beren and Lúthien ('The Tale of Tinúviel' in *The Book of Lost Tales*) and turned it into a long poem in octosyllabic couplets: 'The Gest of Beren and Lúthien' or 'The Lay of Leithian' (*Lays*, pp. 150–329). Before the end of 1929, Tolkien gave Lewis 'The Lay of Leithian' to read. In a letter to Tolkien, Lewis wrote that he stayed up all night reading it and praised the work for its reality and mythical value (*Lays*, p. 151). Lewis also provided Tolkien with a list of suggested changes, somewhat parodying academic commentary on real medieval manuscripts (see *Lays*, pp. 315–29).

As for the rest of Tolkien's mythology, it was expanding from a 'Sketch of the mythology' in 1926 (which itself was a re-conceived version of the earlier 'Book of Lost Tales') to the 'Quenta Noldorinwa' (*Shaping*, pp. 76–218), which would establish the main narrative of the mythology before he started work on *The Lord of the Rings*. Associated with the 'Quenta' is Tolkien's first 'Silmarillion' map, which geographically represented the secondary world Tolkien had created by this time and included place-names in Qenya and Noldorin (*Shaping*, pp. 219–34). In the early 1930s Tolkien also started to express his mythology using a historical-chronicle form, similar to works such as *The Anglo-Saxon Chronicle*. Tolkien worked on 'The Earliest Annals of Valinor' and 'The Earliest Annals of Beleriand', partially translating both from English into Anglo-Saxon (*Shaping*, pp. 262–341).

In addition to the emerging 'Silmarillion' mythology, Tolkien also worked on several other creative projects in prose and poetry. In 1927, he published two poems under the general title: 'Adventures in Unnatural History and Medieval Metres, being The Freaks of Fisiologus' in *The Stapeldon Magazine*, a publication of Exeter College, which Tolkien attended as an undergraduate. In these poems, Tolkien parodies the medieval bestiary by juxtaposing different semi-mythical creatures in playful verse. In 1930, Tolkien also completed work on his *Lay of Aotrou and Itroun*, a poem modelled on a medieval Breton lay.

In the early 1930s, both just before and very soon after the delivery of 'A Secret Vice', Tolkien was also occupied by two other key literary compositions. First, drawing on his own lectures on the Old Norse Eddas and Sagas*, Tolkien composed two original poems: 'Völsungakviða en nýja' (The New Lay of the Völsungs) and 'Guðrúnarkviða en nýja' (The New Lay of Gudrún)†. His aim was to attempt a reconstruction of the story of the Volsungs, to include new material covering that which was missing in the Norse Sagas (see *Sigurd*, pp. 5–12). Second, Tolkien composed an alliterative Arthurian poem. As Christopher Tolkien's 2013 edition of *The Fall of Arthur*

---

* Folios 50 verso and 51 verso of the 'Secret Vice' materials contain Tolkien's notes on the *Völsunga saga*, possibly for a lecture.

† Published in 2009 by Christopher Tolkien as *The Legend of Sigurd and Gudrún*.

illustrates, Tolkien attempted to link the departure of Arthur and Lancelot to the West with his own 'Silmarillion' mythology (see *Fall of Arthur*, pp. 123–68).

Tolkien also wrote poems for his children during that period. By 1931, a doll owned by his children had inspired him to start writing poems and, interestingly, construct a small piece of prose, about the whimsical character Tom Bombadil (see *Bombadil*). Another of his children's toys inspired *Roverandom*, a tale he eventually wrote down in 1927. It was also during this period that Tolkien also started sending his children letters from 'Father Christmas' each December. In 1928, Tolkien composed a cycle of poems incorporating fantasy and satire called the 'Tales and Songs of Bimble Bay' (see Anderson 2003, pp. 309–11). During this period, Tolkien also wrote *Farmer Giles of Ham*, a comic tale about a dragon and his bumbling adversary set in the medieval villages around Oxford. Yet another dragon tale emerges sometime around, or shortly after, the summer of 1930 (see Rateliff 2007, p. xiii); a tale that Tolkien told his children, and with which they were so enraptured, that in the early 1930s he was compelled to put on to paper. *The Hobbit* was published in 1937. It gave the reading public the smallest glimpse of the, by now quite vast, mythology that Tolkien had been developing up to this time.

'A Secret Vice' is, therefore, a key text, from a key period, that not only brings together Tolkien's *academic* and *creative* work on language, but is probably the first occasion at which Tolkien spoke publicly, if a little cryptically, about his entirely private mythology and secondary world. It could be argued that at 9 pm on 29 November 1931, Tolkien revealed to the world the 'coeval and congenital' arts of world-building and language invention – the crux of his creative endeavours and literary success.

'A Secret Vice' and the Larger Context

Tolkien was not the first author to invent languages for fiction. 'Art-langs' (as they are often termed) are found already during the early modern period in the 'traveller's tale', a genre that flourished alongside real-world exploration, and which gave writers such as Thomas More, Bishop Godwin, Cyrano de Bergerac, Gabriel de Foigny and Jonathan Swift the opportunity to invent fictional peoples in fantastic locations (often imaginary islands) speaking exotic languages (see Fimi 2008, p. 94; Higgins 2015, pp. 43–7). In *The Book of Lost Tales* Tolkien himself used the 'traveller's tale' trope to connect his emerging mythology to England's re-imagined past, by having the mariner Ottor Wǽfre (later, Eriol) travel to the Lonely Isle and encounter the exiled Elves who speak the earliest forms of Tolkien's invented languages. Jonathan Swift's *Gulliver's Travels* (1726) became an important landmark in the early use of language invention. He created names, place-names and phrases in several imaginative languages spoken by the residents of the fantastical places Lemuel Gulliver is ship-wrecked upon. As revealed in this volume, Tolkien referred to Swift in 'A Secret Vice' and made notes on his impressions of Swift's language invention (see pp. 86–7).

In the Victorian period the traveller's tale became linked to several of the earliest works of science fiction such as Edgar Allan Poe's *The Narrative of Arthur Gordon Pym of Nantucket* (1838), Percy Greg's *Across the Zodiac: The Story of A Wrecked Record* (1880) and Edward Bulwer, Lord Lytton's *The Coming Race* (1871), all of which included specimens of fictional languages (see Higgins, 2015, pp. 47–8). Bulwer-Lytton's use of language invention is especially interesting as the imaginary language of Vril-ya 'is constructed as an extrapolation from the accepted truths of the linguistic science of the time' (Yaguello 1991, p. 45). Indeed, Bulwer-Lytton dedicated this dystopian novel to the Oxford philologist Max Müller whose ideas on language development and decay Bulwer-Lytton imaginatively incorporated into the invented history of the language of Vril-ya.

Tolkien's linguistic invention also responded to his times in similar ways. As outlined above, 'A Secret Vice' was first conceived and delivered at an important period in the continuum of Tolkien's literary and academic work. This time also represented a particular social, historical and intellectual moment. The late 1920s and early 1930s saw the last promising flowering of International Auxiliary Languages, important trends and changes in linguistic theories, and language experimentation in art, mainly represented by Modernism as a literary movement. 'A Secret Vice' and Tolkien's accompanying drafts and papers seem to engage with, and respond to, these contemporary trends and contexts.

Creating a new language, or seeking to re-create a long-lost *ideal* language, has been an important – yet often overlooked – aspect of the Western tradition. Medieval scholars attempted to recover, or rediscover, the language of Adam, the primeval 'perfect' language lost via the sin of Babel, according to the Judaeo-Christian tradition (see Eco 1995; Yaguello 1991, pp. 10–14). Many brilliant minds of the seventeenth and eighteenth centuries, such as Francis Lodwick*, Gottfried Leibniz, John Wilkins and George Dalgarno, endeavoured to construct a universal *philosophical* language, which would be based on a logical and mathematical description of the universe and would

---

* Lodwick also invented a 'Universal Alphabet' which has many common elements with Tolkien's *tengwar* (Allan 1978, pp. 276–9; Fimi 2008, pp. 112–13).

eliminate the perceived imprecise, disorganized and unsystematic disposition of natural languages (see Okrent 2009, 19–75). By the nineteenth century, the *a priori* (made from scratch) languages of the previous era had given way to *international* languages, constructed *a posteriori* (using elements of existing natural languages), also termed *auxiliary* as they were meant to serve a more utilitarian role: to facilitate communication at a time when the world was seemingly becoming smaller. The acronym IAL (International Auxiliary Language) was used for a plethora of such projects, the proliferation of which in the late nineteenth and early twentieth centuries reached 'epidemic proportions' (Yaguello 1991, p. 52). As Yaguello notes:

the period 1880–1914 witnessed frenzied activity in this sphere. Monnerot-Dumaine lists 145 projects for this period alone, which amounts to almost 40% of the total of 368 [invented] languages spread over four centuries. (1991, p. 53)

As Fimi has discussed (2008, pp. 93–5), it was in the midst of this intellectual climate that Tolkien started working on the earliest stages of his legendarium, and the 'coeval and congenital' construction of his fictional languages. Some of the most significant IALs from that period, of which Tolkien will have been aware, included *Volapük, Esperanto, Ido*, and *Novial* (see *Letters*, p. 231). Two of them are referred to in Tolkien's writings presented in this volume.

Ludwik Lazarus Zamenhof's IAL was published in 1887 under the pseudonym 'Doktoro Esperanto' (Doctor Hopeful), which eventually gave his language its name. His 'hope' was that his language would unite humanity and bring in a new era of international tolerance and respect. *Esperanto* was designed to be intelligible by Europeans with very little study. According to D.B. Gregor, speakers of Romance languages could immediately recognize 80% of *Esperanto*, speakers of Germanic languages 63%, and speakers of Slavic languages 17% (Gregor 1982, p. 28). It boasted a grammar with no exceptions and relied on a system of roots and affixes. Esperanto acquired a strong following and continues to be spoken by around one million people today (Smith 2011, p. 38).

Esperanto's success inevitably led to many imitators, reformers and improvers. *Novial* (*nov-* 'new' + IAL) was such a project by prominent linguist Otto Jespersen. Jespersen chose roots for Novial 'according to the principle of greatest internationality' and used auxiliary verbs in a similar way to English (Smith 2011, p. 39). There are two instances in Tolkien's published writings where he referred to Novial (pretty much unfavourably – see below) but he mentioned *Esperanto* by itself on a number of occasions in his published corpus, including in 'A Secret Vice', in his preamble to introduce the subject of imaginary languages.

Tolkien seems to have learnt Esperanto by 1909, as suggested by evidence contained in a small notebook he kept at the time called the 'Book of the Foxrook'.* In this notebook the seventeen-year-old Tolkien outlined a secret code consisting of a 'rune-like phonetic alphabet' and 'a sizeable number of ideographic symbols', which Tolkien called 'monographs', each of which represented an entire word (Smith and Wynne 2000, p. 30). This 'Private Scout Code' (as Tolkien called it) worked, presumably, by using the 'monographs' for most words, and

---

* During that period, Tolkien's life was revolving around the Birmingham Oratory to which his guardian, the Catholic Priest Father Francis Morgan, belonged. It may be significant that the Catholic Church seems to have always welcomed the Esperanto movement. In 1906 Esperanto received the first papal blessing, while in 1910 the International Catholic Esperanto Union (IKUE) was founded (see Ulrich 2002, pp. 36–44).

the rune-like alphabet (each enclosed in a cartouche) 'to spell personal names or words for which a monograph was not available' (ibid., p. 31). He appears to have invented a writing system that combined a phonetic alphabet (clearly associated with the sounds of English) and ideographic symbols. The instructions on the sounds that his rune-like alphabet represented, though, are in pure Esperanto, and he maintains that – with a few exceptions – his alphabet is used to spell phonetically 'as in Esperanto' (ibid., p. 31).*

Tolkien refers to the Esperanto World Congress of 1930 in 'A Secret Vice' (p. 4) and a year later he had become a member of the Board of Honorary Advisers to the Education Committee of the British Esperanto Association. In a letter supporting Esperanto, published in *The British Esperantist* in May 1932, he claimed that he wasn't a 'practical Esperantist' but that '25 years ago I learned and have not forgotten its grammar and structure, and at one time read a fair amount written in it' (cited in Smith and Wynne 2000, p. 35)†. In his letter, Tolkien claims

---

* Smith and Wynne (2000) go through every Esperanto word in Tolkien's notebook and outline Esperanto-like words he invented himself, as well as some errors the young man made in his use of Esperanto.

† If Tolkien's reference to '25 years ago' is taken as an accurate memory of when he first learnt Esperanto, then this quotation may be taken as evidence that his original encounter with this IAL was in 1907, two years prior to the 'Book of the Foxrook'. Smith and Wynne point out that this may be the case, citing as possible corroborating evidence the very successful Third Universal Esperanto Congress in Cambridge that year, in which Zamenhof himself took part, which may have inspired Tolkien. Hammond and Scull seem to take the 1907 date as definite in their *Chronology* (p. 13) but Tolkien may simply be using '25 years' as a broad approximation with reference to the period of the 'Book of the Foxrook'. Perhaps this latter hypothesis offers a better explanation for the errors in Tolkien's use of Esperanto, possibly suggesting that he may have been something of a 'beginner'.

that the most important obstacle for any IAL is 'universal prop-agation' adding that one of the main reasons he supports Esperanto is that 'it has already the premier place, has won the widest measure of practical acceptance' (ibid.). These utilitarian concerns notwithstanding, Tolkien also praises Esperanto for its 'individuality', 'euphony', 'coherence and beauty', elements that he attributes to the 'genius of the original author' (ibid.).

Oronzo Cilli (2014) has recently uncovered further links between Tolkien and the Esperanto movement. Tolkien's name is cited as one of the 'patrons' of the 24th British Esperanto Congress which was held in Oxford at Easter 1933. Tolkien is also a co-signatory (together with 23 other academics and edu-cators) of an article on 'The educational value of Esperanto' published in the May 1933 issue of *The British Esperantist*, which seems to have originated in a meeting of the same title recorded in the congress proceedings (see Cilli 2014). Whether Tolkien participated in the 1933 congress or not, he lends his support to a series of statements in favour of Esperanto which broadly agree with his earlier expressed ideas about this IAL: its endur-ance, popularity, and usability. This document concludes that Esperanto should be 'the first language to be studied, after the mother tongue, in the schools of all countries' (cited in Cilli 2014) and also refers to the ever-increasing original literature in Esperanto. This last point is of special importance when it comes to considering Tolkien's next (and last) recorded com-ment on Esperanto, which comes from a letter composed over 20 years later. In 1956, in a draft letter to a certain Mr Thompson, Tolkien delves into his creative process and notes:

> It was just as the 1914 War burst on me that I made the discovery that 'legends' depend on the language to which they belong; but a living language depends equally on the 'legends' which it

conveys by tradition. (For example, that the Greek mythology depends far more on the marvellous aesthetic of its language and so of its nomenclature of persons and places and less on its content than people realize, though of course it depends on both. And *vice versa*. Volapük*, Esperanto, Ido†, Novial, &c &c are dead, far deader than ancient unused languages, because their authors never invented any Esperanto legends.) So though being a philologist by nature and trade (yet one always primarily interested in the aesthetic rather than the functional aspects of language) I began with language, I found myself involved in inventing 'legends' of the same 'taste'. (*Letters*, p. 231)

In contrast to Tolkien's own invented languages, which are indissolubly bound up with the history and legends of the various peoples in his complex secondary world, many IALs divorce language from culture. IALs arguably offer a ready-made linguistic idiom that is simpler, easier to learn, and more logical than natural languages, but may also be perceived as neutral, non-personal, a-historical, standardized, sterile. Okrent notes that this may be the reason why many people talk about IALs with scorn or dismissive humour. An IAL asks us to 'turn away from what makes our languages personal and unique and choose one that is generic

---

* Johann Martin Schleyer's *Volapük* (1879) was one of the earliest of all IALs. It included some *a priori* elements but the bulk of the language was *a posteriori*: notably its vocabulary derived from English, German and the Romance languages (Smith 2011, p. 29). Schleyer was a Roman Catholic priest, and his motto for *Volapük* ('For one humanity, one language!') demonstrates his aspiration that his language would lead to international co-operation and harmony (Smith 2011, p. 26).

† *Ido*, appositely meaning 'Offspring' in *Esperanto*, and proposed by Louis de Beaufront and Louis Couturat (1907), was ostensibly Esperanto with minor amendments (Smith 2011, p. 39).

and universal. It asks us to give up what distinguishes us from the rest of the world for something that makes everyone in the world the same'. They are a 'threat to beauty: neutral, antiseptic, soulless' (Okrent 2009, pp. III–I2). Tolkien's 1956 comment on IALs follows a similar line of argument: he characterizes them as 'dead' languages (a term usually used for languages with no living speakers) because they are not rooted in a cultural context. But, applicable though his comments may be to Volapük, Ido and Novial, they oversimplify the long historical development of Esperanto and the gradual development of an 'Esperanto culture'. The younger Tolkien who co-signed the 1933 article discussed above seems to be more keenly aware of the success of Esperanto over many years, which led to the composition of original literature in this IAL. Okrent (2009) has handled the idea of an 'Esperanto culture' with honesty and sensitivity and has given a colourful and fascinating account of the shared culture of Esperanto speakers when they find themselves in 'Esperantoland' (anywhere in the world Esperanto is spoken – and definitely at congresses and other regular gatherings of Esperanto supporters). She offers evidence of the development of idiomatic language in Esperanto to suit its speakers' shared values, principles and anxieties, and the development of a shared identity beyond national boundaries. The fact that Esperanto has allowed a shared tradition and culture to 'breed' among its speakers, makes it more sympathetic to Tolkien's ideals for invented languages than the older Tolkien is willing to admit.*

---

* Apart from a shared culture, Esperanto came very close to acquiring its own territory. In 1908, only a year before Tolkien's adolescent Esperanto jottings in the 'Book of the Foxrook', 'the tiny neutral state of Moresnet, the orphan of a border dispute between the Netherlands and Prussia, rose up to declare itself the first free Esperanto state of Amikejo (Friendship Place). More than 3 percent of the four thousand inhabitants had learned

The general consensus in Tolkien scholarship is that Tolkien originally expressed admiration for Esperanto but changed his mind later on, or at least lost his original enthusiasm. For example, Hammond and Scull claim that: 'Tolkien's view of artificial languages changed over the years' (*Reader's Guide*, p. 474), using as evidence the 1956 letter quoted above, as well as a few revisions Tolkien made to 'A Secret Vice', as presented by Christopher Tolkien in the original publication of the essay in *The Monsters and the Critics and Other Essays*. Our edition questions the date and interpretation of these particular pencil notes, arguing that they were contemporary with the first delivery of the essay (see p. xxxiv). Moreover, it offers a series of additional comments that Tolkien made on Esperanto and unveils further links between Tolkien and the Esperanto movement. Readers are therefore afforded a more rounded understanding of Tolkien's views on Esperanto at different times.

As noted above, Tolkien mentioned Novial alongside Volapük and Ido in his 1956 letter in order to contrast them with his own invented languages. But there is another cryptic reference to Novial in the same 1932 letter to *The British Esperantist* quoted above. Tolkien writes:

> Actually, it seems to me, too, that technical improvement of the machinery, either aiming at greater simplicity and perspicuity of structure, or at greater internationality, or what not, tends (to judge by recent examples) to destroy the 'humane' or aesthetic aspect of the invented idiom. This apparently unpractical aspect

---

the language (a higher percentage of Esperanto speakers has never been achieved in any other country), and their flag, stamps, coins, and an anthem were ready to go. But in the increasingly tense and nationalistic atmosphere of pre-war Europe, there was no place for a friendship place, and Esperanto never got its piece of terra firma' (Okrent 2009, pp. 81–2).

appears to be largely overlooked by theorists; though I imagine it is not really unpractical, and will have ultimately great influence on the prime matter of universal acceptance. N**, for instance, is ingenious, and easier than Esperanto, but hideous – 'factory product' is written all over it, or rather, "made of spare parts" – and it has no gleam of the individuality, coherence and beauty, which appear in the great natural idioms, and which do appear to a considerable degree (probably as high a degree as is possible in an artificial idiom) in Esperanto . . . (quoted in Smith and Wynne 2000, p. 36).

Smith and Wynne are right to point out that the only IAL Tolkien can be plausibly referring to in this letter is Novial, which Jespersen had released in 1928. They also hypothesize that the reason for Tolkien's discrete reference ('N**', rather than naming it in full) was his reluctance to criticize a fellow-philologist and eminent scholar – and a colleague that Tolkien admired for his work on linguistics and whose books he had praised in his reviews for the *Year's Work in English Studies* a few years earlier (*YWES V*, pp. 28–32, 52; *YWES VI*, p. 56). But Jespersen's principles for an IAL, applied in Novial and outlined a year later in an article, seem to have jarred with Tolkien's investment in the aesthetic qualities of invented languages, even if they were to be used as IALs, as evident from the letter above. Jespersen's principles included the use of:

a) pre-existing international roots (i.e. creation of an *a posteriori* IAL)
b) a phonetic system which should be as simple as possible, in order not to hinder non-European nations
c) the Roman alphabet (based on the fact that it is the best-known one worldwide)

d) spelling that is simplified and as easy as possible

e) grammatical material from existing languages and no grammatical irregularities whatsoever

f) tenses that are formed by short auxiliaries – apart from the past tense that would be denoted by a different ending to the present (see Jespersen 1929)

Jespersen's objective, quite evidently, was an IAL that would be regular, logical, and easy to pronounce and use for speakers of any language of the world. That Tolkien was referring to Novial in the letter above is therefore even clearer when his criticism concentrates on the exact elements Jespersen aspired to: 'greater simplicity and perspicuity of structure' or 'greater internationality' – elements that Tolkien felt were to the detriment of individuality, coherence and beauty, and made Novial sterile, contrived and colourless. This edition offers more evidence of Tolkien's thinking about Novial.

Tolkien's language invention, therefore, seems to respond to contemporary IALs. Indeed, as he reflects in 'A Secret Vice', his early efforts of language invention were often associated with communities of (child) speakers seeking an instrument of (playful) communication. But Tolkien swiftly progressed from invented languages as *communication* to invented languages as *art*. It is, then, unsurprising that Tolkien also responded to the *aesthetics* of contemporary IALs, as noted above. This response was not only limited to the 'beauty in word-form' but also took into account the sense of 'fitness' between sound and meaning (see above, pp. 24, 25). The latter corresponds to the notion of 'sound symbolism', the idea that there is a direct relationship between the sounds making up a word and its meaning.

Sound symbolism* may range from onomatopoeia, to particular qualities of objects consistently represented by certain sounds (e.g. the association of the 'ee' sound in English with smallness, as in 'wee', 'little', 'tiny'), to clusters of sounds more conventionally associated with certain meanings (e.g. the initial 'gl' in 'glisten', 'glitter', 'glow' indicates similar meanings).† The story of sound symbolism goes back to theological and mystical writings of ancient and medieval times (see Magnus 1999; Etzel 1983), among which Plato's dialogue *Cratylus* (c. late fourth century BC) is still considered as one of the foundation texts for subsequent scholarship. In this work, Cratylus takes the view that a word's meaning is determined by its sound. Against him speaks Hermogenes, who maintains that there is no relationship between word and sound. These two extreme views are often called the *naturalist* vs. *conventionalist* perspectives on sound and meaning (see Magnus 2013, pp. 192–3; Morgan 1995, p. xxiii). Finally, Socrates argues against both of these diametrically opposed views, taking a position somewhere in between by claiming that language should be, sometimes can be, but is not always mimetic (Morgan 1995, p. xxv). In the early modern period Gottfried Leibniz and John Locke took opposing positions in the naturalist vs. conventionalist extremes of this debate, while by the nineteenth century, Wilhelm von Humboldt had developed a typology of sounds symbolism (see Magnus 2013, 194–5, 196).

---

* Alternative terminology includes 'phonetic symbolism', 'linguistic iconism', 'phonosemantics', and in French and other continental scholarship 'mimologique'/mimology (see Magnus 2001, p. 190; Körtvélyessy 2015, p. 147; Genette 1995).

† These three categories make up the main typology of sound symbolism: 'imitative', 'synesthetic' and 'conventional' sound symbolism (see Hinton et al 1994, pp. 1–6).

In the early twentieth century, Saussure's famous pronouncement 'the sign is arbitrary' became extremely influential. The advent of structural linguistics led to approaching language as a self-autonomous semiotic system and Saussure's conventionalist thesis became a central orthodoxy in modern linguistics (see Anderson 1998, pp. 15–21). Nevertheless, the discussion about sound symbolism continued in the twentieth century, but the focus now shifted to empirical methods of investigating this phenomenon. Magnus (2013, pp. 197–201) distinguishes between two categories of empirical studies: 1) studies in the correlation between sound and meaning in existing vocabulary of real languages; and 2) studies of native speakers' intuitions about nonsense words or isolated sounds. In the early twentieth century two linguists (whose work Tolkien knew and to whose ideas he seems to be responding in his notes to 'A Secret Vice') contributed to each of these two directions of research: Leonard Bloomfield and Edward Sapir.

Bloomfield seems to have originally supported sound symbolism of a sort. In his doctoral dissertation, *A Semasiological Differentiation in Germanic Secondary Ablaut*, he compiled an extensive (arguably nearly complete) list of Germanic roots and demonstrated that words derived from them displayed vowel gradation (ablaut) which was essentially sound-symbolic in nature. Bloomfield saw the pitch of the vowel and the meaning of the word as directly related: high-pitched vowels (e.g. 'i') represent 'clear' and 'shrill' sounds and denote 'fine, small, bright, flashing, quick, sharp, clear-cut objects or actions' while low-pitched vowels express 'low, muffled, rumbling, bubbling sounds and dull, loose, swaying, hobbling, slovenly, muddy, underhand, clumsy actions' (Bloomfield 1909, p. 8). For an example in English, note the change in sound and meaning between the pairs 'flip-flop', or 'snip-snap'. Bloomfield's study has been described as groundbreaking because of its comprehensiveness: rather than picking and choosing particular roots and their vowel gradations that would prove his theory, Bloomfield aimed at a complete list of all Germanic roots and therefore demonstrated the pervasiveness of this type of sound symbolism in Germanic languages (see Magnus 2013, pp. 198–9). However, by the 1920s Bloomfield had changed his mind. In his critique of works by Edward Sapir and Otto Jespersen he rejected any view that may give credence to the idea that 'psychology' or 'mental processes' may affect language, and he was especially critical of Jespersen's work on sound symbolism (see Falk 1992, pp. 471–6).

Otto Jespersen was perhaps 'the most adamant phonosemanticist prior to the Second World War' (Magnus 2001, p. 22). His seminal work *Language: Its Nature, Development and Origin* (1922) included an entire chapter on sound symbolism, as well as a chapter on the origins of human language, and he actually saw affinities between the two. Jespersen explores sound symbolism not only in onomatopoeia, but also in the way sound may be associated with the appearance of things (e.g. light or dark), states of mind, size and distance (1922, pp. 398–406). His 'general considerations' about sound symbolism make a number of important points, including the fact that 'no language utilizes sound symbolism to its full extent'; and that sound symbolism is not only limited to 'primitive' language but continues to be operative as language develops to this day and may be responsible for the way certain words have changed in time, ending up being more 'expressive' (Jespersen 1922, pp. 406–11).

Edward Sapir seems to have followed the opposite trajectory to that of Bloomfield. In his earlier works he appears sceptical of the notion of sound symbolism (see Anderson 1998, pp. 65–7) but he later modified his position following a series of psycho-linguistic experiments. He famously gave the subjects of his studies two meaningless words – 'mil' and 'mal' – and asked them to choose which one they would associate with a big table and which with a small. The great majority felt that 'mil' would be the right term for the small table and 'mal' for the big one (Sapir 1929). Sapir's studies paved the way for further psycholin-guistic experiments in the 1930s (see Magnus 2013, p. 201).

Tolkien was aware of Bloomfield's and Sapir's work, and he also knew Jespersen's research very well. All three linguists were roughly of his generation – though all three were more senior to him in terms of experience and academic career. Tolkien refers to them a handful of times in his published corpus but most references are concentrated in the three review pieces on 'Philology: General Works', which he wrote for the *Year's Work in English Studies*, volumes 4–6 (1924–7).[*] Jespersen had not published his work on Novial by that time, but Bloomfield was already against sound symbolism, as demonstrated by his essay 'Einiges vom germanischen Wortschatz'[†], which Tolkien reviewed. In this article Bloomfield is concerned with irregular-ities of Germanic vocabulary, and comments on the fact that a large part of the Germanic vocabulary cannot be accounted for by regular sound laws. He rejects, however, *Lautsymbolik* ('sound symbolism') as the reason for this phenomenon. He associates sound symbolism with naive and emotional approaches to the study of language and insists, instead, on other regular linguistic phenomena (such as assimilation and

---

[*] Tolkien also refers to Bloomfield in *Finn and Hengest: The Fragment and the Episode*, published in 1982, but based on Tolkien's lectures in the early 1930s.

[†] The essay was included in *Germanica: Eduard Sievers zum 75. Geburtstage* a Festschrift for the German philologist Eduard Sievers.

analogy) that should be considered rigorously and methodically to answer this research question. Bloomfield, however, does assign meaning to 'clusters' of sounds. He notes that Germanic vocabulary seems to have initial, final and medial sound-groups that are 'morphologically active', and cites groups of words such as flame, flare, flash, flicker, etc.; bash, clash, crash, gnash, etc.; and nitter, natter, nutter respectively. Tolkien's review is quick to notice Bloomfield's slight self-contradiction here:

> *Lautsymbolik* comes in for scorn; but by it is apparently meant creation in the void (without pre-existing models developed regularly), and 'spontaneous gemination' and the like. *Lautsymbolik* of the sort that attaches significance to sound-groups developed at first mechanically, and extends their use, is of the essence of the article. Why it should more than once be called 'naïve' is not made clear. Once you admit even naïve feeling, however vague, for the significance of certain groups of sounds you have *Lautsymbolik* of a sort, and it requires attention. The grouping of words which is here offered both in rhyming and in alliterative series (*flame, flare, flash*, &c.; *flash*; *splash*, &c.) brings out many interesting points of word-formation. (*YWES* VI, pp. 37–8)

This is the only instance in his published writings prior to 'A Secret Vice' where Tolkien comments on sound symbolism directly (he uses the German term *Lautsymbolik* after Bloomfield's article). Clearly, by the mid-1920s he was interested in sound symbolism and its effect on language change and development and he boldly criticized one of the linguistic authorities of the time who rejected its significance. In this volume, Tolkien's own thoughts on sound symbolism are presented in his hitherto unpublished 'Essay on Phonetic Symbolism' (see pp. 63–71).

Although not strictly writing on sound symbolism, Owen Barfield was very influential for Tolkien through his work on related notions. Barfield was at the periphery of the Inklings and his book *Poetic Diction* (1928) proved to be a significant influence on Tolkien's thinking and his mythopoeia, as it has been brilliantly discussed by Verlyn Flieger (2002). Barfield's main thesis was the interconnectedness of language, consciousness and perception. He argued that in its beginnings language did not distinguish between literal and metaphorical meanings of words:

> Each word embodied an 'ancient semantic unity' of meaning that has over time divided and subdivided into ever narrower, more precise, and often more abstract units of meaning. He gave as an example the Greek word *pneuma*, now of necessity translated variously as 'wind,' 'breath,' or 'spirit' depending on the context but originally encompassing all of these aspects, whose interlocking meanings were perceived as essentially the same. (Flieger 2007, p. 50)

Language, therefore, was originally more mythical. In Barfield's theory, 'words had originally themselves been mini-myths, embodying a view of reality in which experienced phenomena were at one and the same time physical and spiritual' (Phelpstead 2014, p. 84).

In *Poetic Diction* Barfield did not examine sound and meaning (and their relation) as an integral part of this 'ancient semantic unity', but in chapter 2 he made this parenthetical comment:

> The sound of language is crucially relevant to its poetic meaning, indeed, owing to the peculiar relation of the vocal organs

to the rest of the body, it is relevant even to those correspond-
ences which will be considered later under the heading of
'metaphor'. It has a bearing, too, on the essentially *active* nature
of the poetic consciousness, which is one of the findings of this
book. But the subject is an extremely subtle and delicate one
and, thanks to the changes of form which words undergo in the
course of their history, is particularly difficult to discuss theor-
etically and illustrate with examples. Though they may be
indistinguishable in practice, topically it is possible to distin-
guish the intellectual element in poetic meaning from the tonal;
and where there is more than one topic, it is reasonable to deal
with one at a time. Accordingly I have, for the purpose of this
book, considered sound as lying outside the province of poetic
diction, properly so called, and it will not be further discussed.
(1973, pp. 47–8)

But in later works Barfield went on to identify the breaking of
what he considered to be the original, direct relationship
between sound and meaning as part of the same process of
dividing and subdividing the 'ancient semantic unity' of words.
In *Saving the Appearances* (1957) he writes:

The split between sound and meaning – for their relation in any
modern language is no more than vestigial – is one aspect of the
ever-widening gulf between outer and inner, phenomenon and
name, thing and thought . . . Certainly those who have any feel-
ing for sound-symbolism, and who wish to develop it, will be
well advised to ponder [word-roots]. They may find, in the con-
sonantal element in language, vestiges of those forces which
brought into being the external structure of nature, including
the body of man; and, in the original vowel-sounds, the expres-
sion of that inner life of feeling and memory which constitutes

his soul. It is the two together which have made possible, by first physically and then verbally embodying it, his personal intelligence. (1988, pp. 123–4)

Barfield's ideas, therefore, only hinted at in *Poetic Diction* and developed much more fully in later books, encompass the notion of sound symbolism, although his understanding of the phenomenon is less grounded in experimental work of contemporary philologists and linguists and more in the older Western tradition of Cratylism and the pursuit of an ideal original language. It is not, therefore, surprising that Magnus, in her recent brief history of sound symbolism, lists Barfield as one of a number of 'leading philosophers' of the late nineteenth and early twentieth century who 'took issue with structuralism or the schism implied between signifier and signified' (2013, p. 203). Barfield's influence on Tolkien is well-documented (see Flieger 1981 and 2002) and this volume records additional references made by Tolkien to his fellow Inkling's work in the context of Tolkien's discussion of sound symbolism.

Apart from the context of IALs and contemporary linguistic ideas about sound symbolism, the early twentieth century saw radical experimentation with *language as art* by Modernism and related avant-garde literary movements. In the same way that the Modernists reacted against mimesis by challenging the notion that art or literature can (or should) represent reality, they also 'turned away from the ideal of a language that would offer a transparent window onto reality' (Lewis 2007, p. 4). Poets and novelists during that period often attempted to 'break' language, strip it of its conventions, re-create it, and reach a new level of communication that would be more direct but also more complex, subjective and subconscious. At the extreme end of that spectrum 'sound poetry' and the 'new languages' created by different brands of Futurism* stand side by side with the new linguistic idioms of Modernist writers such as Gertrude Stein and James Joyce. Both Stein and Joyce published repeatedly in Eugene Jolas' avant-garde periodical *transition* and both are mentioned by Tolkien in his notes to 'A Secret Vice' (see pp. 100 and 91 respectively).

Gertrude Stein experimented with different genres and styles but her avant-garde poetry foregrounded the sound, rhythm and music of language, rather than its meaning (Shaughnessy 2007, p. 44). Her notorious line 'a rose is a rose is a rose is a rose', which appeared in several of her works, plays with repetition and musicality on many different levels. There is a sense that this is a fragment of an ever-repeated sequence that never ends but loops into itself – in *Lectures in America* Stein said that she made it 'into a ring' (1936, p. 231) – but also the continuous repetition of the same word ultimately divorces sense and meaning and imbues the word with a freshness and newness that it has lost (see Stein 1947, pp. v–vi). Stein's use of repetition was, therefore, a conscious technique to allow one of the most basic qualities of language, the 'rhythm and melody of words' (Scheunemann 2000, p. 102), to dominate over meaning and to let the word be born afresh. Her reversal of the customary subordination of sound to meaning allowed for the composition of poetry based on the musicality of words, rather than any conventional use of words to 'mean something'. This artistic choice earned her a reputation for being obscure, unintelligible or even absurd (for contemporary reviews see Leick 2009). As Scheunemann has eloquently put it: 'the isolation and exposure

---

* Fimi (2008, pp. 90–1) and Smith (2007) have discussed Tolkien's linguistic invention in the context of avant-garde movements such as the Russian Futurists' *zaum*, Italian futurism and the Dada poets.

of the sound qualities of words and word associations was the risk Gertrude Stein took in the face of poetic tradition' (2000, p. 105).

Stein's notoriety as a 'difficult' writer, whom some greeted as a genius and others dismissed as a farce, had provoked C.S. Lewis' voluble indignation, which would have put her on Tolkien's radar. In 1926 she was invited to Oxford for a lecture, an event orchestrated by Edith Sitwell and promoted by Harold Acton (Dydo 2003, pp. 77–132). Both Stein's *The Autobiography of Alice B. Toklas* (Toklas was Stein's lifelong partner) and C.S. Lewis' diary record an incident at the lecture, when Stein – when challenged by an Oxford don – gave a witty reply (see Stein 1966, pp. 253–4; Lewis 1991, p. 413). Lewis' diary reveals that the don was actually Lord David Cecil, then Fellow and Lecturer in Modern History at Wadham College. Lewis did not attend the lecture himself – the incident was narrated to him by Nevill Coghill who had been present. Both Lord Cecil and Coghill were members of the Inklings, the informal literary society to which both Lewis and Tolkien belonged, and who met regularly to read and critique each others' creative works.

The opinion of the Johnson Society on Gertrude Stein can be gauged by the minutes of their 17 June 1928 meeting (only two days before Tolkien attended the Society's Annual Dinner as a guest), during which Ralph Withington Church gave a paper on Stein:

This woman, it appears, has made it her life's work to bring out the true beauty of words by divorcing them from all meaning. Mr. Church seemed well-acquainted with this subject, and read many amusing extracts to the Society. In fact the Society appeared to see in the extracts, a humour which the authoress could never have intended. And in the discussion which followed, the general opinion of the Society was that Miss Stein had achieved but half her purpose. That is to say, she had undoubtedly succeeded in depriving words of all meaning, but the result was not only unbeautiful, but even utterly ridiculous. (Johnson Society Minute Book, PMB/R/6/1/6 1927–9)

As illustrated by Tolkien's notes accompanying 'A Secret Vice' (p. 100), Tolkien did engage with Stein's poetry when commenting on the relationship between sound and meaning in linguistic invention.

James Joyce was another Modernist figure who made an equally notorious name for himself as radical, experimental, obscure, and the inventor of his own linguistic idiom. It is not an exaggeration to say that for Joyce – especially in his later writings – literature was an experiment in language. After the stream-of-consciousness and inventive use of onomatopoeia in *Ulysses* (1922), Joyce embarked on his most ambitious project, *Finnegans Wake* (1939), which was known for years as *Work in Progress*, and fragments of which were published in *transition* and other publications between 1924 and 1938. Joyce's language in this work was to be deliberately complex and opaque, resonating with the novel's night-time setting. As he declared, he wanted to 'invade the world of dreams' and therefore had to 'put the language to sleep' (cited in Ellmann 1983, p. 546). Joyce's novel is deliberately polyglot – John Bishop (1986) has identified Joyce's playful use of over forty languages and dialects – and includes a plethora of neologisms based on punning, onomatopoeia, portmanteau techniques, and manipulating homonyms and etymologies, as well as creative and often humorous distortion of grammar (for representative examples of Joyce's linguistic invention see Watt 2011, pp. 169–73).

Joyce's linguistic experimentation has often been discussed

as an attempt at a 'universal language'. Indeed, Joyce himself had expressed his wish for 'a language which is above all languages, a language to which all will do service. I cannot express myself in English without enclosing myself in a tradition' (cited in Zweig 1943, p. 275). This discourse situates Joyce within the late nineteenth- and early twentieth-century proliferation of IALs and the tradition of universal and auxiliary languages. Indeed, it has been shown that Joyce was particularly fascinated by the 'problem of Babel' and that *Finnegans Wake* contains a number of references and allusions to IALs such as Esperanto, Volapük, and Ido (see Shaw Sailer 1999; Schotter 2010, pp. 90–4). Joyce was also interested in the theories on the origin of language, and was particularly attracted to the idea that human speech originated in gestures, especially after attending lectures by Marcel Jousse and reading the work of Sir Richard Paget (Milesi 2008, p. 474). Tolkien also read Paget, as his comments in the 'Essay on Phonetic Symbolism' in this volume show. In addition, although Joyce's writing shares a number of interests and preoccupations with the IAL movement, like Tolkien he did not strive for a communication language but an artistic one. As the political climate darkened in Europe with the rise of Fascism and Nazism, Joyce was interested in a language that would move beyond nationalism and would embrace a cosmopolitan view. As Schotter has eloquently put it, *Finnegans Wake* showed that 'the dream of a pure language is unreachable':

> Joyce provides in his own version of a universal language not the solution to the problem of Babel but Babel itself: a radically impure cacophony of different languages that is only an exaggerated form of the polyglot and arbitrary nature of all communication. (Schotter 2010, p. 100)

That Tolkien and his circle knew of avant-garde and Modernist poets and novelists, including Stein and Joyce, is evident from a number of comments in C.S. Lewis' diaries, letters and notes. In a 1935 letter, Lewis refers derogatorily to T.S. Eliot and his 'natural friends and allies, the Steins, the Pounds and *hoc genus omne*, the Parisian riff-raff of denationalized Irishmen and Americans who have perhaps given Western Europe her death wound' (2004, p. 164). In his own copy of his 1933 allegorical novel *The Pilgrim's Regress*, in the part where his main character encounters the 'gibberish' literature of the 'lunatic twenties', C.S. Lewis added a handwritten note: 'Try the works of Gertrude Stein or Joyce's Anna Livia Pluribella [*sic*] or the sur-realists, Dadaists etc.' (2014, p. 44). The new material edited in this volume reveals some of Tolkien's thoughts on this experi-mental period of Modernist writing, but, unlike Lewis (who objected on political and moral grounds), he chooses to focus on a critique of the artistic qualities of Joyce and Stein.

'A Secret Vice', its attendant 'Essay on Phonetic Symbolism', and the associated notes and drafts published in this volume reveal Tolkien in a key moment of his academic and creative career, in the process of finding his way amidst contemporary forces of tradition and revolution. Imaginary languages had featured in fantastic fiction for centuries, but Tolkien was one of only a very few practitioners who fleshed them out in great detail, and who was perhaps unique in attempting to use them to write poetry. Numerous schemes for International Auxiliary Languages were fighting for supremacy, but Tolkien aspired towards private invention, focusing on aesthetics rather than universality and simplicity. Sound symbolism was becoming a marginal field, as Saussurian linguistics were gradually gaining the status of orthodoxy, but Tolkien defended it and attempted to explicate and exploit its potential. Avant-garde and modernist writers were experimenting with language in ways that seemed often anarchic and unstructured, but Tolkien continued to strive for language as art within a strict philological system. This volume, therefore, affirms once more Tolkien's characterization by his official biographer, Humphrey Carpenter, as: 'a man of antitheses' (*Biography*, p. 95).

PART I

PART I

'A Secret Vice'

The essay (MS Tolkien 24, folios 10–24, 26–36, 38–42) is written in black ink on 'Oxford paper'* using two examination booklets (of 14 and 26 pages, respectively), as well as loose pages torn out of examination booklets. Folios 35 and 39, which contain translations of two Elvish poems, are typescripts on much flimsier, brownish paper. There are numerous pencil and ink emendations throughout the essay, as well as longer additional sections in pencil with indications of where they should be inserted. Most of these emendations and additions seem contemporary, apart from three instances (see Introduction, p. xxxiv) that may indicate a later delivery of this paper.

---

* Apart from folios 1, 35, 39 and 53, all of Tolkien's drafts and notes are written on what is conventionally called 'Oxford paper', described by Christopher Tolkien as:

> the paper of good quality that my father used for many years in all his writing (University lectures, *The Silmarillion*, *The Lord of the Rings*, etc.) in ink or pencil (i.e. when not typing): this plain paper was supplied to him by the Examination Schools at Oxford University, being the unused pages of the booklets of paper provided for examination candidates. (*Lays*, p. 81)

Tolkien started using 'Oxford paper' in the summer of 1924 (when he was still in Leeds, but acting as an external examiner for the University of Oxford) and continued using it for many years.

3

The title of the essay in the manuscript is 'A Hobby for the Home'. In his 1983 edition of the essay Christopher Tolkien wrote:

> The ironic title in the manuscript itself is *A Hobby for the Home*
> . . . but my father referred to it in 1967 by a different title: 'The amusement of making up languages is very common among children (I once wrote a paper on it, called *A Secret Vice*)' (*The Letters of J.R.R. Tolkien*, p. 374). The words 'a secret vice' occur in the essay; and I have adopted this title. (*Monsters*, pp. 3–4)

The Johnson Society minutes (see pp. xxxii–xxxiii) show that Tolkien did indeed use 'A Secret Vice' as his title when he first delivered the paper and we have, therefore, kept the title in this edition.

We have presented all the material included in the folios above, including pencil emendations and additions, in an attempt to reconstruct the essay as close as possible to the form it was in when first delivered. For example, folios 24r and 24v on the Fonwegian language, written in pencil and inserted as a loose leaf inside one of the examination booklets, were not included in the original edition of the essay. However, the minutes of the Johnson Society show that Tolkien did read those inserted pages (see above, pp. xxxii–xxxiii) so we have included them where Tolkien indicates.

A Hobby for the Home[1]

Some of you[2] may have heard that there was ~~recently~~ a year or more ago a {illeg} Congress in Oxford, an Esperanto[3] Congress[4]; or you may not have heard.	In other words <u>home-made</u> or Invented languages[8] Esperanto. La Onklino de Charlie

I heard – because I was invited to it by a certain Mr McCallum or Macallumo[5] to see a performance of La Onklino de Charlie[6].

Personally I am a believer in an "artificial" language, at any rate for Europe – a believer that is in its desirability, as the one thing antecedently necessary for uniting Europe, before it is swallowed by America[7]/non-Europe; as well as for many other good reasons – a believer in its possibility because the history of the world seems to exhibit, as far as I know it, both an increase in human control (or influence upon) the uncontrollable, and a progressive widening of the range of more or less uniform languages. Also I particularly like Esperanto, not least because it is the creation ultimately of one man, not a philologist, and is therefore something like a "human language bereft of the inconveniences due to too many successive cooks" – which is as good a description of the ideal artificial language (in a particular sense) as I can give.

In other words home-made or Invented languages[8]

Now I believe in the possibility of an artificial language – I am no longer so sure that it would be a good thing. But at least it is possible, and perhaps probable. For the general trend has been towards an increase of human control over (or deliberate interference at with at any rate) the what was previously 'instinct' or traditional.

Anyway I think that Esperanto per se has much to be said for it – it is likeable. Largely because it was in the main the creation or artifact of one man (not a philologist) but something of an artist.)
"A human language bereft of the inconveniences of one to too many successive cooks."

At present I think we should be likely to get an inhumane language without any cooks at all – their place being taken by nutrition experts and dehydrators.

No doubt the Esperantist propaganda touched on all these points. ~~I wasn't there, so~~ I cannot say. But it is not important, because my concern is not with that kind of artificial language at all. You must tolerate the stealthy approach. It is habitual. But in any case my real subject tonight is a stealthy subject. ~~Rather a bashful matter.~~ Indeed nothing less embarrassing than the <u>revealing</u>/unveiling in public of a secret vice. Had I boldly and brazenly begun right on my theme I might have called my paper a plea for a New Art, ~~or at any rate~~ a New Game ~~or at least/perhaps the public reception of an ancient one.~~[9] ~~I might have done so, with a disgusting arrogance not justified by the possible advertisement value of such a title~~, if occasional and painful confidences had not given me grave cause to suspect that the vice, though secret, is ~~not unique~~ common, and the art (or game), if new at all, has at least been discovered by a good many other people independently.

The practitioners are all so ~~shy and ashamed~~ bashful however, that they ~~never~~ hardly ever show their works to one another, so none of ~~us~~ them know who are the geniuses at the game, or who are the splendid "primitives" whose neglected works, found in old drawers[10], may possibly be purchased at great price (not from the authors, or their heirs and assigns!) for American museums, in after days when the 'art' has become acknowledged. I won't say 'general'! – it is too arduous and slow: I doubt if any devotee could produce more than one real masterpiece, plus at most a few brilliant sketches or outlines, in a life-time.

I shall never forget a little man – smaller than myself – whose name I have forgotten[11], revealing himself by accident as a devotee, in a moment of extreme ennui, in a dirty wet marquee filled with trestle tables smelling of stale mutton fat, crowded with (mostly) depressed and wet creatures. We were listening to somebody lecturing on map-reading, or camp-hygiene, or the art of sticking a fellow through without (in defiance of Kipling[12]) bothering who God sent the bill to; rather we were trying to avoid listening, though the Guards' English, and voice, is penetrating. The man next to me said suddenly in a dreamy voice: "Yes, I think I shall express the accusative case by a prefix!"[13]

A memorable remark! Of course by repeating it I have let the cat, so carefully hidden, out of its bag, or at least revealed the whiskers.[14] But we won't bother about that for a moment. Just consider the splendour of the words! "I shall express the accusative case." Magnificent! Not "it is expressed", nor even the more shambling "it is sometimes expressed", nor the grim "you must learn how it is expressed". What a pondering of alternatives within one's choice before the final decision in favour of the daring and unusual prefix, so personal, so attractive; the final solution of some element in a design that had hitherto proved refractory. Here were no base considerations of the 'practical', the easiest for the 'modern mind', or for the million – only a question of taste, a satisfaction of a personal pleasure, a private sense of fitness.

As he said this word the little man's smile was full of a great delight, as of a poet or painter seeing suddenly the solution of a hitherto clumsy passage. Yet he proved as close as an oyster. I never gathered any further details of his secret grammar; and military arrangements soon separated us never to meet again (up to now at any rate). But I gathered that this queer creature – ever afterwards a little bashful after inadvertently revealing his secret – cheered and comforted himself in the tedium and squalors of 'training under canvas' by composing a language, a personal system and symphony that no one else was to study or to hear. Whether he did this in his head (as only the great masters can), or on paper, I never knew. It is incidentally one of the attractions of this hobby that it needs so little apparatus! How far he ever proceeded in his composition, I never heard. Probably he was blown to bits in the very moment of deciding upon some ravishing method of indicating the subjunctive. The Great War was/Wars are not favourable to delicate pleasures.

But he was not the only one of his kind.[15] I would venture to assert that, even if I did not know it from direct evidence. It is inevitable, if you "educate" most people, many of them more or less artistic or creative, not solely receptive, by teaching them languages. Few philologists even are devoid of the making instinct – but they often know but one thing well; they must build with the bricks they have.[16] There must be a secret hierarchy of such folk. Where the little man stood in this, I do not know. High I should guess. What range of accomplishment there is among these hidden craftsmen, I can only surmise – and I surmise the range runs, if one only knew, from the crude chalk-scrawl of the village schoolboy to the heights of palaeolithic or bushman art (or beyond). Its development to perfection must none the less certainly be prevented by its solitariness, the lack of interchange, open rivalry, study or imitation of other's technique.

I give no names. I have made small efforts of research. I use as evidence merely some of the material that sheer chance has brought my way. So I give no names. All One of the persons whose secrets (not in all cases divulged wholly) is dead, but the others are alive.[17]

I have had some glimpses of the lower stages. I knew two people once[18] – two is a rare phenomenon – who constructed a language called Animalic almost entirely out of English animal bird and fish names; and they conversed in it fluently to the dismay of the bystanders. I was never fully instructed in it, nor a proper animalic-speaker,[19] but I remember out of the rag-bag of memory that <u>dog nightingale woodpecker forty</u> meant "<u>you are an ass</u>". Crude (in some ways) in the extreme. There is here, again a rare phenomenon, a complete absence of phonematic[20] invention which at least in embryo is usually an element in all such constructions. <u>Donkey</u> was 40 in the numeral system, whence <u>forty</u> acquired a converse meaning.

I had better say at once: "Don't mistake the cat which is slowly emerging from the bag!" I am not dealing with {illeg} that curious phenomenon 'nursery-languages'[21], as they are sometimes called – the people I quote were of course young children and went on to more advanced forms later – some of which languages are ~~entirely esoteric~~ as individual and peculiar as this one, while some acquire a wide distribution and pass from nursery to nursery and school to school, even country to country, in a mysterious way without any adult assistance, though new learners usually believe themselves in possession of a secret. Like the insertion type of "language"[22]. I can still remember my surprise after acquiring with assiduous practice great fluency in one of these "languages" my horror at ~~hear~~ overhearing two entirely strange boys[23] conversing in it. This is a very interesting matter – connected with cant, argot, jargon[24], and all kinds of human undergrowth, and also with games and many other things. But I am not concerned with it now, even though it has affinities with my topic. A purely linguistic element, which is my subject, is found sometimes even in this childish make-believe. The distinction – the test by which one can discriminate between the species I am talking about, from the species I am leaving aside – lies, I think, in this. The argot-groups are not primarily concerned at all with relations of sound and sense[25]; they are not (except casually and accidentally like real languages) artistic – if it is possible to be artistic inadvertently. They are 'practical', more severely so even than real languages, actually or in pretence. They satisfy either the need for limiting one's intelligibility within circles whose bounds you can more or less control or estimate, or the fun found in this limitation. They serve the needs of a secret and persecuted society, or the queer instinct for pretending you belong to one. The means of being 'practical' are crude – they are usually grabbed randomly by the young or by ~~the~~ rude persons without apprenticeship in a difficult art, often with little aptitude for it or interest in it.

That being so, I would not have quoted the "animalic"-children, if I had not discovered that secrecy was no part of their object. Anyone could learn the tongue who bothered. It was not used deliberately to bewilder or to hoodwink the adult. A new element comes in. The fun must have been found in some ~~other th~~ thing else than the secret-society or the initiation business. Where? I imagine in using the linguistic faculty, strong in children and excited by lessons consisting largely of new tongues, purely for amusement and pleasure. There is something attractive in the thought – indeed I think it gives food for various thoughts, and I hope that, though I shall hardly indicate them, they <u>will come out in discussion</u>/occur to my hearers.

The faculty for making visible marks is sufficiently latent in all for them (caught young enough) to learn, more or less, at least one graphic system, with severely practical object. It is more highly developed in others, and may lead not only to heights of illumination and calligraphy for sheer pleasure, but it is doubtless allied in many ways to drawing.[26][27]

The linguistic faculty – for making so-called articulate noises – is sufficiently latent in all for them (caught young as they always are) to learn, more or less, at least one language with merely/or mainly practical object. It is more highly developed in others, and may lead not only to polyglots but to poets; ~~or else~~ to savourers of linguistic flavours, to learners ~~of~~ and users of tongues who take pleasure in the exercise. And it is allied to a higher art of which I am speaking, and which I ~~shall~~ perhaps ~~eventually define~~ had better now define.[28] An art for which life is not long enough[29], indeed: the construction of imaginary languages in full or outline for amusement, for the pleasure of the constructor or even conceivably of any critic that might occur.[30] For though I have made much of the secrecy of the practice of this art, it is an inessential, and an accidental product of circumstances. Individualistic as are the makers, seeking a personal expression and satisfaction, they are artists and incomplete without an audience. Though like this or any other society of philologists[31] they may be aware that their goods have not a wide popular appeal or a market, they would not be averse to a ~~sympathetic~~ competent and unbiased hearing in camera.

But I have somewhat interrupted my argument, and anticipated the end of my line of development which was to lead from the cruder beginnings to the highest stages. I have seen glimpses of higher stages than animalic. As one proceeds higher in the scale doubtless diverse ramifications begin: 'language' has more than one aspect, which may be specially developed.[32] I can imagine developments I have never met.

A good example of a further stage was provided by one of the Animalic community – the other (notably not the originator) dropped off and became interested in drawing and design.[33] The other developed an idiom called Nevbosh, or the 'New Nonsense'.[34] It still made, as these play-languages will, some pretence at being a means of limited communication – that is, in the lower stages the differentiation between the argot-group and the art-group is imperfect. That is where I came in. I was a member of the Nevbosh-speaking world.

Though I never confessed it, I was older in secret vice[35] (secret only because apparently bereft of the hope of communication or criticism), if not in years, than the Nevbosh originator. Yet, though I shared in the vocabulary, and did something to affect the spelling of this idiom, it remained a usable business, and intended to be. It did become too difficult to talk with Animalic fluency – because games cannot take up all one's time with Latin and mathematics and such things forced upon one's notice – but it was good enough for letters, and even bursts of doggerel song. I believe I could still write down a much bigger vocabulary of Nevbosh than Busbecq recorded for Crimean Gothic[36], though more than 20/almost 40[37] years have gone by since it became a dead language. But I can only remember entire one idiotic connected fragment:

> Dar fўs ma vel gom co palt "hoc
> Pys go iskili far maino woc?
> Pro si go fys do roc de
> Do cat ym maino bocte
> De volt fac soc ma taimful gyróc!"[38]

Now this vocabulary, if ever I were foolish enough to write it down, and these fragments, of which the only surviving native can still supply a translation, are crude – not in the extreme, but still crude. I have not sophisticated them. But they already provide quite instructive matter for consideration. It is not yet sufficiently developed to present the points of interest for a ~~literary~~ learned[39] society which I hope may yet arise; [the interest is still chiefly discoverable by the scientific and the philological, and so only a side-line with me tonight.] But I will touch on it, because it will I think be found not altogether foreign to the present purpose of this absurd paper.

~~Some~~ One of the points I see ~~are here~~ is this: – What happens when people try to invent 'new words' (groups of sounds) to represent familiar notions. Whether the notion becomes in any way affected or not we will leave aside – it is negligible at any rate in a case like Nevbosh, which is entirely dominated by an established natural idiom. This 'invention' is probably always going on – to the distraction of 'etymology', which more or less assumes, or used to assume, creation once for all in a distant past.[40] Such a special case as Nevbosh, supported by others like it, of which no doubt one could find many examples if one knew where to look, might throw light on this interesting problem, which is really part of a more advanced etymology and semantic. In traditional languages invention is more often seen undeveloped, severely limited by the weight of tradition, or alloyed with other linguistic processes, and finds outlet chiefly in the modification of existing sound-groups to "fit" the sense (this 'fit' begs a large question, but never mind), or even modification of sense to 'fit' the sound. In this way, in either case, 'new words' are really made – since a 'word' being is a group of sounds temporarily more or less fixed + an associated notion more or less defined and fixed in itself and in its relation to the sound-symbol. Made not created. There is in historic language, traditional or artificial, no pure creation in the void.

In Nevbosh we see, of course, no real breaking away from 'English' or the native traditional language. Its notions – their associations with certain sounds, even their inherited and accidental confusions; their range and limits – are preserved. Do is 'to', and a prefixed inflexion marking the infinitive. Pro is 'for, four', and the conjunction 'for'. And so on. This part is not then of any interest. Only on the phonematic side is here much interest. What directed the choice of non-traditional sound-groups to represent the traditional ones (with their sense-associations) as perfectly as equivalent counters?

Clearly 'phonetic predilection' – artistic phonetic expression[41] – played as yet a very small part owing to the domination of the native language, which still kept <u>Nevbosh</u> almost in the stage of a 'code'. The native language constantly appears with what at first sight appears casual unsystematic and arbitrary alteration. Yet even here there is a certain interest – little or no phonetic knowledge was possessed by its makers, and yet there appears an unconscious appreciation of certain elementary phonetic relations: alteration is mainly limited to shifting within a defined series of consonants, say for example the dentals: d, t, þ, ð, etc. <u>Dar</u>/there; <u>do</u>/to; <u>cat</u>/get; <u>volt</u>/would. Or where this is broken as in <u>ym</u>/in, we have recognition of the fact that <u>m/n</u>, though technically made ~~in~~ at different contact points, have in their nasality and resonance a similarity which overrides the ~~other~~ more mechanical distinction – a fact which is reflected, shall we say, both in the case of <u>m/n</u> interchange in real languages (such as Greek), or in my inability to feel greatly wounded by <u>m/n</u> assonances in a rhyming poem.[42]

The influence of learnt languages – or since all are learnt, better lesson-languages – is unfortunately prominent in this <u>Nevbosh</u> example, an influence which weakens its interest in some respects, though it brings in an additional point for consideration. The intricate blending of the native with the later-learnt is, for one thing, curious. The foreign, too, shows the same arbitrary alteration within phonetic limits as the native. So <u>roc</u>/'rogo' ask; <u>go</u>/'ego' I; <u>vel</u> ('<u>vieil</u>, <u>vieux</u>' old); <u>gom</u>/'homo' man[43] – the ancient Germanic languages did not contribute[44]; <u>pys</u>/can – from French; <u>si</u>/if – pure plagiarism; ~~far 'fero'/carry~~ <u>pal</u>/'parler' speak, say; <u>taim</u>/'timeo' fear; and so on. Blending is seen in – volt/'volo, vouloir' + 'will, would'; <u>fys</u>/'fui' + 'was', was, were; <u>co</u>/'qui, who' + 'who'; <u>far</u>/'fero' bear, carry. And in a curious example: <u>woc</u> is both the native word reversed, and connected with vacca, vache[45] (as I happen to remember that this is actually the case); but it bred the beginnings of a code-like system, dependent on English, whereby native -ow > -oc, a sort of primitive and arbitrary sound-law: hoc/how; gyroc/row.

Perhaps it was not worth going into so much so deeply. A code is not an interesting subject. Only those words which have no obvious association in traditional or school-learnt languages would possess a deeper interest – and one would have to possess a very great number of documented examples to learn anything of value from them, more than the arousing of a passing curiosity.

In this connexion iski-li "possibly" is odd. Who can analyse it? I can also remember the word lint/'quick clever nimble', and it is interesting, because I know it was adopted because the relation between the sounds lint[46] and the idea proposed for association with them, gave pleasure. Here is the beginning of a new and exciting element. Certainly, just as in real languages, the 'word' once thus established, though owing its being to this pleasure, this sense of fitness, quickly became a mere chance symbol dominated by the notion not the relation and its circle of association, not by the relation of sound and sense[47] – thus it was soon used for mental quickness, and finally the normally {sic} Nevbosh idiom for "learn" was catlint (become 'lint'), and for "teach" faclint (make 'lint').

Generally speaking, however, only the incipient pleasure found in linguistic invention, in getting free from the necessarily limited scope invention has for any individual within a traditional sphere, makes these rude fragments of interest.

This idea of using the linguistic faculty for amusement is however deeply interesting to me. I may be like an opium-smoker seeking a moral or medical or artistic defence for his habit. I don't think so. The instinct for 'linguistic invention'

– the fitting of notion to oral symbol, and <u>pleasure in contem-</u>
<u>plating the new relation established</u> – is rational, and not
perverted. In these invented languages the pleasure is more
keen than it can be even in learning a new language – keen
though it is to some people in that case – because more per-
sonal and fresh, more open to experiment of trial and error.
And it is capable of developing into an art, with refinement of
the construction of the symbol, and with greater nicety in the
choice of notional-range.

Certainly it is the <u>contemplation</u> of the relation between
sound and notion which is a main source of pleasure. We see it
in an alloyed form in the peculiar keenness of the delight schol-
ars have in poetry or fine prose in a foreign language, almost
before they have mastered that language, and long after they
have become reasonably familiar with it.[48] Certainly in the case
of dead languages no scholar can ever reach the full position of
a native with regard to the purely notional side of the language
he studies, nor possess and feel all the undercurrents of conno-
tation from period to period which words possess. His
compensation remains a great freshness of perception of the
word-form. Thus, even seen darkly through the distorting glass
of our ignorance of the details of Greek pronunciation, our
appreciation of the splendour of Homeric Greek in word-form
is possibly keener, or more conscious, than it was to a Greek,
much else of other elements of poetry though we may miss. The
same is true of Anglo-Saxon. It is one of the real arguments for
devoted study of ancient languages. Nor does it mean self-
deception – we need not believe we are feeling something that
was not there; we are <u>only</u> in a position to see some things
better at a distance, others more dimly.

The very word-form itself, of course, even unassociated with
notions, is capable of giving pleasure – a perception of beauty,

which if of a minor sort is not more foolish and irrational than being sensitive to the line of a hill, light and shade, or colour. Greek, Finnish, Welsh (to name at random languages which have a very characteristic and in their different ways beautiful word-form, readily seizable by the sensitive at first sight) are capable of producing this pleasure. I have heard others independently voice my own feeling that the Welsh names on coal-trucks have stirred a sense of beauty, provided you have the barest knowledge of Welsh spelling sufficient for them to cease to be jumbles of letters.[49]

There is purely artistic pleasure, keen and of a high order, in studying a Gothic dictionary from this point of view; and from it a <u>part</u>, one element, of the pleasure which might have been gained from the resplendent 'lost Gothic' poetry, may still be recaptured.[50]

It is then in the <u>refinement of the word-form</u> that the next progress above the Nevbosh stage must consist. Most unfortunately above this 2nd still crude Nevbosh-stage the development tends to dive underground, and to be difficult to document with examples. Most of the addicts reach their maximum of linguistic playfulness, and their interest is swamped by greater ones, they take to poetry or prose or painting, or else it is overwhelmed by mere pastimes (cricket, meccano[51], and such like footle) or crushed by cares and tasks. A few go on, but they become shy, be ashamed of spending the precious commodity of time for their private pleasure, and higher developments are locked in secret places. The obviously unremunerative character of the hobby is against it – it can earn no prizes, win no competitions (as yet) – make no birthday presents for aunts (as a rule) – earn no scholarship, fellowship, or worship. It is also often – like poetry – contrary to conscience, and duty; its pursuit is snatched from hours due to self-advancement, or to bread, or to employers.

It is difficult to get evidence of higher stages. [This must be my excuse for becoming more and more autobiographical – regretfully, and from no arrogance. I should much prefer the greater objectivity of studying other people's efforts.] The crude Nevbosh was a 'language' in a fuller sense than things we are coming to. It was intended in theory for speaking, and writing, between one person and another. It was shared. Each element had to be accepted by more than one to become current, to become part of Nevbosh at all. It was therefore hampered in 'symmetry', either grammatical or phonetic, as traditional languages are. Only the handing on to a wider group, going on during a long time, could have produced in it some of those effects of partially achieved and overlaid symmetries which mark all the traditional human tongues. Nevbosh represented the ~~lowest~~ highest common linguistic capacity of a small group, not the best that could be produced by ~~one of its~~ its best member. It remained unfreed from the purely communicative aspect of language – the one that seems usually supposed to be the real germ and original impulse of language. But I doubt this exceedingly; as much as one doubts a poet's sole object, even primary one, being to talk in a special way to other people.

The communication factor has been a very powerful in directing the development of language; but the ~~factor that played a~~ more individual & personal factor ~~one of this is the factor~~ – pleasure in articulate sound, and in the symbolic use of it, independent of communication though constantly in fact entangled with it – must not be forgotten for a moment.

Naffarin – is the next stage ~~I will briefly~~ of which I have evidence to put before you – shows very clear ~~signs~~ signs of a development in this direction. It was a purely private production, [partly overlapping the last stages of Nevbosh, never circulated (though not for lack of the wish). It has long since been foolishly destroyed, but I can remember more than enough, accurately and without sophistication, for my present purpose.] One set of individual predilections – governed powerfully as is inevitable by accidents of knowledge, but not made by them – comes to some sort of expression. The phonetic system is limited, and is no longer that of the native language, except that it does not contain elements entirely alien to it; there is a grammar, again a matter of predilection and choice of means. [With regard to phonetic system one may say in an aside that the absence of alien elements is not of first-class importance; a very alien word-form could be constructed out of purely English phonetic elements; since it is as much in habitual sequences and combinations as in individual 'phonemes' or sound-units that a language, or a language-maker, ~~expresses its peculiarity~~ achieves individuality. A fact which can be readily appreciated by turning English backwards – phonetically, not by spelling. Such a 'native' word as scratch, becomes štærks, each 'phoneme' being perfectly native, the total entirely foreign[52] owing to the fact that English rarely has the sequence št – only when it is clearly analysable as š + suffix (crushed), and never initially; never has ær + consonant. It is this fact, of course, which gives English scholars' 'Greek' still a Greek phonetic character – a representation of Greek with other counters, as Nevbosh was a representation of English on the notional side – in spite of its purely English detail.

Such scholars need not, however, be unduly comforted – their usage still misrepresents Greek in vital ways, and might be improved vastly still using only English phonetic detail.]

To return – I will give you a brief sample of Naffarin.

O Naffarínos cutá vu navru cangor
luttos ca vúna tiéranar,
dana maga tíer ce vru encá vún' farta
once ya merúta vúna maxt' amámen.

I don't mean to subject this example to the tédious consider-
ation of origins which I inflicted upon you and Nevbosh.
Etymologically, as you would see if I bothered to translate, it
has no greater interest than ~~Nevbosh; vrú 'ever' – [a curiously~~
~~predominant word association in my languages, which is always~~
~~pushing its way in (a case of early fixation of individual associa-~~
~~tion, I suppose, which cannot now be got rid of)]~~ very possibly
cutá – ever is certainly part of vrú and cedo, cesso of cutár[53] – is
the only word of interest from this point of view.[54] [In inventing
languages one inevitably develops a style and even mannerisms
– even though it is one of the elements of the game to study
how a linguistic 'style' is composed.]

In Naffarin the influences – outside English, and beyond a
nascent purely individual element – are Latin and Spanish, in
sound-choices and combinations, in general word form. These
influences no longer preclude the expression of personal taste,
because French and German and Greek, say, all of which were
available, were not used or not much used; phonetic taste in indi-
vidual phonemes is also present; though chiefly negatively: in the
absence of certain sounds familiar in English (w, þ, š, ž, etc.).
Allowing oneself to be influenced by one pattern rather than
another is a choice. Naffarin is definitely a product of a 'Romance'
period. But we need not trouble about this specimen any more.

Here I will interpose some material – which will save this
paper from being too autobiographical. I recently became pos-
sessed by accident of some secret documents[55] – a grammar and
glossary and some sentences in the Fonwegian language spoken

apparently in the island of Fonway.[56] Now this specimen, though much less sophisticated in some ways than Naffarin, deserves to be placed ~~at~~ after it as being 'higher' – because it is more original. Dependent as it is for the 'scheme' of its grammar on the "learned" languages ~~like~~ Latin and French, both its phonetic structure and its mechanism is peculiar and individual, and appears to owe nothing to English, French and Latin. It clearly illustrates my point about s̆rærks above. Its sounds are English, its grammar largely Latin, but it remains individual. A 'character' runs through it as clearly as it can in say one person's handwriting using the traditional cursive handwriting of Europe. (Read vocabulary through)

					neuter
Pronouns	ib	noh,	won,	wone	wonos
	imer,	noher,	woner,	wonere,	wonoser

Note ib, imer, but noh, noher (English, French, Latin)
note relation of genders of 3rd person (Lat)
but wonoser and this fact that feminine –e goes at end, but
os neuter always next stem is carried out through all the
gram[57]

Thus con making		con	cone	conos
	gen	conis	conise	conosis
	pl	coner	conere	conoser
		coneris	conerise	conoseris

The 'agglutinative' idea[58] is attained by a 'maker' who had no practical experience of anything but inflected languages. Also the 'invention' – the association of sound or symbol & sense is singularly free from pressure of tradition. Practically nowhere can one perceive the association implied by English, French or

Latin directing the choice. Thus in grammar _is_ genitive is sole example & that very differently employed.

In a vocabulary of some 250 words extant there are only about 9 + 12 (21) that have derivative suggestion: ac and (but that is really = both); momor death agroul field, caphill, episti letter, amosa love, pase peace, regens i.e. que[e], nausi sailor taxtos perhaps pen foot, pont gate, dubu many, malle mother (but father is pugos) lauka praise, pullfriga plough, rogis red, ruxa rouse, glabsi sword, teplose time, usut useful, vase voice

A noteworthy feature is the trisyllabic character: ~~ac and~~; butonge arrow; wegolang good, fugollink-a Guild, tillabif- conquer especially in compound or durable nature: wedfor enemy, wag-nose fill up, tundadulla fear lugwolla guard

But even in such a moderate effort as this, it is as difficult as in a fully formed traditional communication language to analyse and state precisely in what the character lies – in what its Fonwegianness is shown. A few obvious traits such as fon – in fonlogos book; fonwulla attack;

wun wunkslita avoid cun cunfordos carriage
ll fonwulla attack, huntilla despise, didula defeat, tundadulla
fear regullarum horse, lugwolla I guard, fuballala teach.

Absence of "onomatopoeia" – laugh is Pindulla, sing is cablea

The whole is slightly reminiscent in fact of 'the Swiftian' character as seen in Scraps vouchsafed of the Lilliputian, Blefuscanudian, and Brobdingnagian idioms.[59] We may leave out his horse language[60] – as that was not intended to be human and is largely an eye joke (and not very good)[61]. Swift makes some effort to differentiate the Lilliput type from the Brobdingnag – but while one would (unless one knew ones "Gulliver" by heart, which would not prove anything) not be able unerringly to assign many words to pygmy or giant, a general Swiftian character pervades ~~all~~ the whole.

From here onwards you must forgive pure egotism. Further examples must be drawn solely from isolated private experience. My little man, with his interest in the devices for expression of ~~synt~~ word-relations, in syntactical devices, is too fleeting a glimpse to use. And I should like to represent to you the interest and delight of this domestic and private art, of many facets, as well as to suggest the points for discussion which it raises (other of course than the question whether practitioners are quite right in their heads).

Practice produces skill here, as in other more useful or more exalted pursuits; but skill need not be expended solely on canvases ~~80 feet square~~ of 80 square feet; there are smaller experiments and sketches.[62] I will offer some specimens of at least one language that has in the opinion of, or rather to the feeling of, its constructor reached a highish level both of beauty in word-form considered abstractly, and of ingenuity in the relations of symbol and sense, not to mention its elaborate grammatical arrangements, nor its hypothetical historical background (a necessary thing as a constructor finds in the end both for the satisfactory construction of the word-form, and for the giving of an illusion of coherence and unity to the whole).

Here would be the place, perhaps, before submitting the specimens, to consider what pleasure or instruction or both the individual maker of a play-language in elaborated form derives from his useless hobby. And then, what points worthy of discussion his efforts may suggest ~~for the observer~~ to the observer, or critic. I originally embarked on this odd topic because I somewhat dimly grasped at questions which did seem to me to arise, of interest not only to students of language, but to ~~the consideration of~~ those considering rather mythology, poetry, art. As one suggestion, I might fling out the ~~fact~~ view that for perfect construction of an art-language it is found necessary to construct at least in outline a mythology concomitant. Not solely because some pieces of verse will inevitably be part of the (more or less) completed structure, but because the making of language and mythology are related functions (coeval and congenital, not related as disease to health, or as by-product to main manufacture);[63] to give your language an individual flavour, it must have woven into it the threads of an individual mythology, individual while working within the scheme of natural human mythopoeia, as your word-form may be individual while working within the hackneyed limits of human, even European, phonetics. The converse indeed is true, your language construction will <u>breed</u> a mythology.

If I only toss out, or lightly suggest these points it is due both to the fact of my slender grasp of the things involved, and to the original intention of the paper, which is simply to provoke discussion.

To turn to another aspect of language-construction: I am personally most interested perhaps in word-form in itself, and in word-form in relation to meaning (so-called phonetic fitness) than in any other department. Of great interest to me is the attempt to disentangle – if possible – among the elements in this predilection and in this association (1) the personal from (2) the traditional. The two are doubtless much interwoven – the <u>personal</u> being possibly (though it is not proven) linked to the traditional in normal lives by heredity, as well as by the immediate and daily pressure of the traditional upon the personal from earliest childhood. The <u>personal</u>, too, is doubtless divisible again into (a) what is peculiar to one individual, even when all the weighty influence of his native language and of other languages he has learnt in some degree, has been accounted for; and (b) what is common to human beings, or to larger or smaller groups of them – both latent in individuals and expressed and operative in his own or any language. The really <u>peculiar</u> comes seldom to expression, unless the individual is given a measure of release by the practice of this odd art, beyond perhaps loose predilections for given words or rhythms or sounds in his own language, or natural liking for this or that language offered for his study rather than for another. Of these well-known facts of experience – including doubtless many of the tricks of style, or individuality in say poetic composition – this <u>individual linguistic character</u>[64] of a person is probably at least in part the explanation.

There are of course various other interests in the hobby. There is the purely philological (a necessary part of the completed whole though it may be developed for its own sake): you may, for instance, construct a pseudo-historical background and deduce the form you have actually decided on from an antecedent and different form (conceived in outline); or you can posit certain tendencies of development and see what sort of form this will produce. In the first case you discover what sort of general tendencies of change produce this a given character; in the second you discover the character produced by given tendencies. Both are interesting, and their exploration gives one a much greater precision and sureness in construction – in the technique in fact of producing an effect you wish to produce for its own sake.

There is the grammatical and logical – a more purely intellectual pursuit: you can (without perhaps concerning yourself so closely, if at all, with the sound-structure, the coherence of the word-form) consider the categories and the relations of words, and the various neat, effective, or ingenious ways in which these can be expressed.[65] In this case you may often devise new and novel, even admirable and effective machinery – though doubtless, simply because the experiment has been tried by others, your human ancestors and relatives, over such a large area for so long a time, you are not likely really to light on anything that in nature or in accident has never anywhere before been discovered or contrived; but that need not bother you. In most cases you won't know; and in any case you will have had, only more consciously and deliberately, and so more keenly, the same creative experience as that of those many unnamed geniuses who have invented the skilful bits of machinery in our traditional languages[66], for the use (and too often the misunderstanding and abuse) of their less skilful fellows.

The time has come now, I suppose, when I can no longer postpone the shame-faced revelation of specimens of my own more considered effort, the best I have done in limited leisure, or by occasional thefts of time, in one direction. The beautiful phonologies, thrown away or mouldering in drawers, arduous if pleasant in construction, the source of what little I know in the matter of phonetic construction based on my own individual predilections, will not interest you.[67] I will offer some pieces of verse in the one language which has been expressly designed to give play to my own most normal phonetic taste[68] – one has moods in this as in all other matters of taste[69], partly due to interior causes, partly to external influences; that is why I say 'normal' – and which has had a long enough history of development to allow of this final fruition: verse. It expresses, and at the same time has fixed, my personal taste. Just as the construction of a mythology expresses at first one's taste, and later conditions one's imagination, and becomes inescapable, so with this language. I can conceive, even sketch, other radically different forms, but always insensibly and inevitably now come back to this one, which must therefore be or have become peculiarly mine.

You must remember that these things were constructed deliberately to be personal, and give private satisfaction – not for scientific experiment, nor yet in expectation of any audience. A consequent weakness is therefore their tendency, too free as they

were from cold exterior criticism, to be 'over-pretty', to be
phonetically and semantically sentimental – while their bare
meaning is probably trivial, not full of red blood or the heat of
the world such as critics demand[70]. Be kindly. For if there is any
virtue in this kind of thing, it is in its intimacy, in its peculiarly
shy individualism. I can sympathize with the shrinking of other
language-makers, as I experience the pain of giving away myself,
which is little lessened by now occurring for a second time.

Oilima Markirya[71]

Man kiluva kirya ninqe
oilima ailinello lúte,
níve qímari ringa ambar
ve maiwin qaine?

Man tiruva kirya ninqe
valkane wilwarindon
lúnelinqe vear
tinwelindon talalínen,
vea falastane,
falma pustane,
rámali tíne,
kalma histane?

Man tenuva súru laustane
taurelasselindon,
ondoli lasse karkane
sildaránar,
minga-ránar,
lanta-ránar,
ve kaivo-kalma;

húro ulmula,
mandu túma?

Man kiluva lómi sangane,
telume lungane
tollalinta ruste,
vea qalume,
mandu yáme,
aira móre ala tinwi
lante no lanta-mindon?

Man tiruva rusta kirya
laiqa ondolissen
nu karne vaiya,
úri nienaite híse
píke assari silde
óresse oilima?

Hui oilima man kiluva,
hui oilimaite?

Oilima Markirya[72]

The Last ~~Ship~~ Ark[73]

Who shall see a white ship
leave the last shore,
the pale phantoms
in her cold bosom
like gulls wailing?

Who shall heed a white ship,
vague as a butterfly,

in the flowing sea
on wings like stars,
the sea surging,
the foam blowing,
the wings shining,
the light fading?

Who shall hear the wind roaring
like leaves of forests;
the white rocks snarling
in the moon gleaming,
in the moon waning,
in the moon falling
a corpse-candle;
the storm mumbling,
the abyss moving?

Who shall see the clouds gather,
the heavens bending
upon crumbling hills,
the sea heaving,
the abyss yawning,
the old darkness
beyond the stars falling
upon fallen towers?

Who shall heed a broken ship
on the green rocks
under red skies,
a bleared[74] sun blinking
on bones gleaming
in the last morning?

Who shall see the last evening?

Nieninqe[75]

Norolinde pirukendea
elle tande Nielikkilis[76],
tanya wende nieninqea
yar I vilya anta miqilis.
I oromandin eller tande
ar wingildin wilwarindeën,
losselie telerinwa,
tálin paptalasselindeën.

This of course has an air or tune to it. The bare literal meaning is intended to be: "Tripping lightly, whirling lightly, thither came little Niéle, that maiden like a snowdrop (Nieninqe) to whom the air gives kisses. The wood-spirits came thither, and the foam-fays like butterflies, the white people of the shores of Elfland, with feet like the music of falling leaves."

or one may have a strict and quantitative metre: –

Earendel[77]

San ninqeruvisse lútier
kiryasse Earendil or vea,
ar laiqali linqi falmari
langon veakiryo kírier;
wingildin o silqelosseën
alkantaméren úrio
kalmainen; i lunte linganer,
tyulmin talalínen aiqalin
kautáron, i súru laustaner.

There upon a white horse sailed Earendel,
upon a ship upon the sea,
and the green wet waves the throat of the sea-ship
clove. The foam-maidens with ~~flower-white h~~ blossom-white
hair made it shine in the lights of the sun; this boat
hummed like a harp-string; the tall masts bent with the
sails; the wind "lausted" (not 'roared' or 'rushed' but made
a windy noise).

Earendel at the Helm.[78]

A white horse in the sun shining,
A white ship in the sea gliding,
Earendel at the helm;
Green waves in the sea moving,
White froth at the prow spuming
Glistening in the sun;
Foam-riders with hair like blossom
And pale arms on the sea's bosom
Chanting wild songs;
Taut ropes like harps tingling,
From far shores a faint singing
Or islands in the deep;
The bent sails in the wind billowing,
The loud wind in the sails bellowing,
The road going on for ever,
Earendel at the helm,
His eyes shining, the sea gliding,
To havens in the West.

Or one can have a fragment from this same mythology, but a
totally different if related language[79]:

Dir avosaith a gwaew hinar
engluid eryd argenaid,
dir Tumledin[80] hin Nebrachar[81]
Yrch[82] methail maethon magradhaid
Damrod[83] dir hanach dalath benn
ven Sirion gar meilien,
gail Luithien[84] heb Eglavar[85]
dir avosaith han Nebrachar

"Like a wind dark through gloomy places the Stonefaces searched the mountains, over Tumledin (the Smooth Valley) from Nebrachar, ~~ores snuffling {illeg} foul creatures scented~~ snuffling goblins smelt out footsteps. Damrod (a hunter) through the vale, down mountain slopes, towards (the river) Sirion went laughing. Lúthien he saw, as a star from Elfland shining over the gloomy places, above Nebrachar."

By way of epilogue, I may say that such fragments, nor even a constructed whole, do not satisfy all the instincts that go to make poetry. It is no part of this paper to plead that such inventions do so; but that they abstract certain of the pleasures of poetic composition (as far as I understand it), & sharpen them by making them more conscious. It is an attenuated emotion, but may be very piercing – this construction of sounds to give pleasure. The human phonetic system is a small-ranged instrument (compared with music as it has now become); yet it is an instrument, and a delicate one.

And with the phonetic pleasure we have blended the more elusive delight of establishing novel relations between symbol and significance, and in contemplating them.

In poetry (of our day – when the use of significant language is so habitual that the word-form is seldom consciously marked, and the associated notions have it almost all their own way) it is the interplay and pattern of the notions adhering to each word that is uppermost. The word-music, according to the nature of the tongue and the skill or ear (conscious or artless) of the poet, runs on heard, but seldom coming to awareness. At rare moments we pause to wonder why a line or couplet produces an effect beyond its significance; we call it the 'authentic magic' of the poet, or some such meaningless expression. So little do we ponder word-form and sound-music, beyond a few hasty observations of its crudest manifestations in rhyme and alliteration, that we are unaware often that the answer is simply that by luck or skill the poet has struck out an air which illuminates the line like a sound of music half-attended to may deepen the significance of some unrelated thing thought or read, while the music ran.

And in a living language this is all the more poignant because the language is not constructed to do this, and only by rare felicity will it say what we wish it to, significantly, and at the same time sing carelessly.

For us departed are the unsophisticated days, when even Homer could pervert a word to suit sound-music; or such merry freedom as one sees in the Kalevala, when a line can be adorned by ~~words~~ phonetic trills – as in enkä lähe Inkerelle, Penkerelle, pänkerelle (Kal. xi 55), or Ihveniä ahvenia, tuimenia, taimenia (Kal. xlviii 100), where pänkerelle, ihveniä, taimenia are 'non-significant', mere notes in a phonetic tune struck to harmonize with penkerelle, or tuimenia which do 'mean' something.[86]

Of course, if you construct your art-language on chosen principles, & in so far as you fix it, and courageously abide by your own rules, resisting the temptation of the supreme despot to alter them for the assistance of this or that technical object on any given occasion, so far you may write poetry of a sort. Of a sort, I would maintain, no further, or very little further, removed from real poetry in full, than is your appreciation of ancient poetry (especially of a fragmentarily recorded poetry such as that of Iceland or ancient England), or your writing of 'verse' in such a foreign idiom. For in these exercises the subtleties of connotation cannot be there: though you give your words meanings, they have not had a real experience of the world in which to acquire the normal richness of human words. Yet in such cases as I have quoted (say Old English or Old Norse), this richness is also absent, equally absent or nearly so. In Latin and Greek even it seems to me that this is more often true than many realize.

But, none the less, as soon as you have fixed even a vague general sense for your words, many of the less subtle but most moving and permanently important of the strokes of poetry are open to you.

For you are the heir of the ages. You have not to grope after the dazzling brilliance of invention of the free adjective, to which all human language has not yet fully attained. You may say

green sun
or dead life.

and set the imagination leaping.

Language has both strengthened imagination and been freed by it. Who shall say whether the free adjective has created images bizarre and beautiful, or the adjective been freed by strange and beautiful ~~images~~ pictures in the mind?[87]

NOTES

1 **A Hobby for the Home:** This alternative title of the essay is also
   inscribed on a brown envelope in which all the 'Secret Vice'
   materials were originally held (part of this envelope has been pre-
   served and is now folio 1 of the folder). Tolkien has also written
   on it: 'Invented Languages' and 'Professor J.R.R. Tolkien'.

2 **Some of you:** As noted in the Introduction (pp. xxxi–xxxiii)
   Tolkien addressed 'A Secret Vice' to members of the Johnson
   Society, Pembroke College, on 29 November 1931. According to
   the minutes those present included: 'The President, the Treasurer,
   The Secretary, Mr. Mellor, Mr. Lee, Mr. Oswald of Wadham, &
   a number of guests of the Society', while the minutes are signed
   by J.M. Booker and E.V.E. White, President (Johnson Society
   Minute Book, PMB/R/6/1/7 1929–37). The Society was founded
   in 1871, its formation inspired by the Pembroke College Fellow
   A.T. Barton, in memory of Samuel Johnson (1709–1784), author
   and lexicographer, and one of the most famous alumni of
   Pembroke College in spite of not actually completing his degree!
   The society's remit was 'the reading of essays on a given subject
   accompanied by free discussion' and was originally an elected
   club (Pembroke College Archives Catalogue). The minute books
   of the Society record a wide range of paper topics. There was the
   occasional paper on Samuel Johnson and other early modern
   British writers (e.g. Jonathan Swift, Thomas Browne and John
   Harington), but also papers on later British poets, novelists and
   playwrights (Matthew Arnold, Thomas Hardy, Rupert Brooke,
   Bernard Shaw), French and Russian novelists (Rabelais, Balzac,
   Gogol and Dostoevsky), a range of American authors (Oliver
   Wendell Holmes, Walt Whitman, Edgar Allan Poe, Sherwood
   Anderson, Eugene O'Neill, Sinclair Lewis), as well as contempo-
   rary Modernists (e.g. Katherine Mansfield and Gertrude Stein).

Other wider topics included the Arthurian legend, Chinese poetry, Japanese colour prints, the Greek islands, the highly contemporary subject of sound in cinema (*The Jazz Singer* being released in 1927), and papers on other intellectual figures such as journalists, critics and scientists (e.g. Christopher Morley, Philip Guedalla, Julian Huxley and T.E. Lawrence, a.k.a. Lawrence of Arabia). The Society met weekly during term time, and also organized dinners in Oxford and London, one of which was memorably held in Samuel Johnson's house in Gough Square, Fleet Street, London, and was graced with the presence of G.K. Chesterton as a guest (Johnson Society Minute Book, PMB/R/6/1/6 1927–9).

3 **Esperanto:** An auxiliary language created between 1872 and 1887 by Ludwik Zamenhof (1859–1917), a Polish ophthalmologist of Lithuanian-Jewish descent who believed that a common language for all would prevent future wars. In youth, he developed the first version of this language, *Lingwe uniwersala*. In 1887 he published his invented language under the pseudonym 'Doktoro Esperanto' (Dr Hopeful) indicating the hope he had for what this common language would do for communication among nations. For Tolkien's background on Esperanto see Introduction, pp. xliii–xlix.

4 **an Esperanto Congress:** The 22nd World Congress of Esperanto (*Universala Kongreso de Esperanto*) was held in Oxford on 2 to 9 August 1930.

5 **by a certain Mr McCallum or Macallumo:** Ronald Buchanan McCallum (1898–1973) was an Oxford don and member of the Inklings. He was elected to a fellowship and tutorship in history at Pembroke College, Oxford in 1925, the same year that Tolkien also became associated with Pembroke as Rawlinson and Bosworth Professor of Anglo-Saxon. McCallum wrote a favourable review of *The Hobbit* (*Pembroke College Record* for 1937–8) and attended meetings of the Inklings from the 1940s (see *Chronology* and Carpenter 1978). He may have been the

inspiration for Alexander Cameron, a minor character in Tolkien's unfinished *The Notion Club Papers* (Bratman 2001). McCallum was involved in the Oxford University Esperanto Club for which he served as Senior Treasurer, and was a speaker during its first public meeting on Tuesday 24th February 1931 on the topic 'Need there be a Language Problem?' (Esperanto Club, Exeter College Archives). Tolkien seems to have rendered his name in Esperanto (Macallumo, -o being the standard masculine ending in Esperanto), perhaps nodding towards McCallum's support for Esperanto, but also to add a humorous tone. His audience, the members of the Pembroke College Johnson Society, certainly knew McCallum as a Fellow of their college, but he had also presented a paper to the Society on G.K. Chesterton on 31st May 1931, six months before Tolkien delivered 'A Secret Vice' (see Introduction, pp. xxxi–xxxii).

6 **La Onklino de Charlie:** The Program of the 22nd Universala Kongreso de Esperanto (Anon. 1930) announces three performances in Esperanto of Brendan Thomas' 1892 farce *Charley's Aunt* as *La Onklino de Charley* (note that Tolkien has misspelt the proper name of the title).

7 **swallowed by America:** In the late 1920s, Tolkien expressed concern about the prominence that American English was gaining over British English and he deplored the idea of a homogenized international English without any sense of individuality. In his 1927 review of G.P. Krapp's book *The English Language in America*, Tolkien noted:

> If on the subject, not unimportant, of the relations of the American and 'British' varieties of English in the most recent period Professor Krapp seems disappointing, it is from the very judicial and non-committal spirit of his utterances and implications, not from his partisanship. But in order to avoid crude prejudice it is not necessary to minimize real differences ... Whether we endeavour to maintain the different varieties of English in

vigorous life now, or in the future seek to restore life after 'English' has become a universalized but dead book-latin, divergence into distinct idioms is ultimately the only thing that will achieve the object.

To the American author, of course, it does not appear so clear as it does to us that the problem is no longer that of the freedom of America and her 'illustrious vernacular', but of the freedom of England. Sir Walter Raleigh in a speech on 'Some Gains of the War' made in February 1918 . . . said: '. . . The greatest gain of all, the entry into the War of America, assures the triumph of our common language and our common ideals.' . . . Some even now are found to criticize the expression 'common language'; more might question 'common ideals' (and without necessarily implying any judgement concerning relative values); but to all it should be apparent that this triumph, if it takes place, is only likely to be 'common' if it is predominantly or wholly American. Whatever be the special destiny and peculiar future splendour of the language of the United States, it is still possible to hope that our fate may be kept distinct. (*YWES* VI, pp. 65–6)

In 'A Secret Vice', one of the reasons Tolkien claims to be supporting Esperanto is its Euro-centric nature, and as a more apposite IAL than a denationalized English. However, he replaced 'America' in his original draft with 'non-Europe' perhaps because he was aware that there were American students in the Johnson Society.

8 **In other words <u>home-made</u> or Invented languages:** The right-hand side of this table presents an alternative opening for the essay, written in pencil and contemporary with its first delivery.

9 **a New Game** ~~or at least/perhaps the public reception of an ancient one:~~ The deleted line shows Tolkien's awareness of the long tradition of language invention, albeit generally little-known and neglected.

10 **whose neglected works, found in old drawers:** By the time

Tolkien first gave this talk he had been privately inventing languages since 1907–8. Given the evidence of linguistic material published posthumously in specialist journals such as *Vinyar Tengwar* and *Parma Eldalamberon*, by the time of this talk's composition Tolkien would have amassed many linguistic documents of his early *Qenya*, *Gnomish* and most recently invented *Noldorin* languages for his mythology (see Introduction: pp. xv–xxx), which may well have been kept in 'old drawers'.

11 **a little man – smaller than myself – whose name I have forgotten:** If this is a real encounter, Tolkien could have met this 'little man' when he was in military training for WWI in July 1915 at Bedford (*Chronology*, p. 71), or in August 1915, when he joined the rest of the 13th Battalion in Lichfield (ibid., p. 72).

12 **in defiance of Kipling:** Tolkien here alludes to the verses:

> Ef you take a sword an' dror it,
> An' go stick a feller thru,
> Guv'ment aint to answer for it,
> God'll send the bill to you.

However, Tolkien misattributes the lines to Kipling. They are, in fact, from American poet James Russell Lowell's *The Biglow Papers*, two series of satirical verses in opposition to the Mexican War and in support of the North during the Civil War, respectively. Patrick Wynne first identified the correct source for Tolkien's quote in a message to the mythsoc online forum on 5 June 2013.

13 **I think I shall express the accusative case by a prefix!:** Some of Tolkien's early Elvish language invention uses a prefix to express case. For example in Gnomish/Goldogrin Nominative *celeb* ('silver') with the addition of a prefix and change of root consonant due to mutation becomes in Genitive *ageleb* (of silver) and in Dative *no-geleb* (to/for silver) (note that there is no accusative case in Gnomish) (*PE* 11, p. 12). Based on limited evidence (*PE* 13, pp. 120–1) vestiges of the prefix to indicate case carried through into Noldorin.

14 **I have let the cat, so carefully hidden, out of its bag:** Idiomatic expression for 'disclosing a guarded secret'. Tolkien seems to have been particularly fond of this idiom, which he also uses in his 1927 review of 'Philology: General Works' ('Some of these cats come out of a strange bag', *YWES* VI, p. 44); as well as in his unfinished *Notion Club Papers* ('if you let your archaic cats out of your private bag', *Sauron Defeated*, p. 242).

15 **But he was not the only one of his kind:** For the tradition of language invention before Tolkien see Introduction, pp. xli–xliii.

16 **but they often know but one thing well; they must build with the bricks they have:** This line chimes with what Tolkien would say about sub-creation and the writing of fantasy in his essay 'On Fairy-stories': 'For creative fantasy is founded upon the hard recognition that things are so in the world as it appears under the sun; on a recognition of fact, but not a slavery to it' (*TOFS*, p. 65).

17 **others are alive:** An interesting statement showing that Tolkien was aware of other past and present language inventors.

18 **I knew two people once:** Tolkien's two cousins: Marjorie (1895–1973) and Mary (1895–1940) Incledon; the daughters of Tolkien's mother's sister Edith Mary ('May') Suffield (1866–1936) who married William Incledon. Starting in childhood (c.1906) Tolkien and his brother Hilary would often visit his two cousins at Barnt Green; a village south-east of Birmingham. Mary Incledon later became godmother to Tolkien's eldest son, John, but died of cancer in 1940 at the age of 45. Marjorie became a painter specializing in watercolours and landscapes. She was one of Tolkien's last visitors when she stayed with him in Oxford in 1972 (see *Letters*, pp. 421–2).

19 **I was never fully instructed in it, nor a proper animalic-speaker:** While Tolkien states that he never became a 'proper' speaker of *Animalic*, he seems to have chosen or been assigned an animal name in that language: Otter. This is evident from his 1909 'Book of the Foxrook', a notebook in which Tolkien outlined a

secret code, which included instructions in Esperanto (see Introduction, pp. xlv–xlvi). Under the title 'Book of the Foxrook', Tolkien adds in Esperanto: 'Privata al LUTRO' (Private to OTTER); if this was Tolkien's name in Animalic, it is significant given the fact that in *The Book of Lost Tales*, dating from some seven years later, Tolkien's fictional informant is the Anglian mariner Eriol, whose original name was *Ottor*, an Old English form of *otter* (Smith and Wynne 2000, p. 33).

20 **phonematic:** A phoneme is a basic unit of sound in a given language; it cannot be analysed into smaller parts and can differentiate words (e.g. /p/ and /b/ in the English words *pat* and *bat*). Tolkien is pointing out here that Animalic was not concerned with inventing new sounds and new words, but rather substituted the meaning of existing words in English.

21 **nursery-languages:** Tolkien here is referring to code languages which children often invent to establish the identity of a specific childhood play group. Such languages deliberately obfuscate words by either a direct replacement of one word for another word that only the group knows the key for (as in Animalic), or distorting words by adding other letters or mixing up the sequence of letters. One of the most popular of these is 'pig-latin', in which English words are deliberately confused by reversing and mixing up their sequence of letters, or placing additional letters in front and at the end of words (e.g. 'pig' is 'igpay'). Other comparable nursery-languages are 'Opish' and 'Turkey Irish', in which clusters of words are added in between the letters of a word to disguise it for all but those who know the code. For example, in 'Opish' an 'op' is added after each consonant, turning the English word 'cat' into 'copatop'. Another more elaborate version of this language is 'Double Dutch' in which each consonant is replaced with a completely different consonant cluster; thus 'how are you' becomes 'hutchowash aruge yubou'.

22 **insertion type of "language":** See note 21 above.

23 **two entirely strange boys:** The minutes of the Johnson Society

mention this story but refer to 'two navvies' rather than two boys (see Introduction, p. xxxiii), a term perhaps more apposite to the context of the next sentence, which refers to cant, argot and jargon.

24 **cant, argot, jargon:** These three terms overlap somewhat and their meanings have changed through time. In contemporary use 'cant' refers to the special phraseology, especially the pompous and inflated language, of a particular class or profession (e.g. the cant of the fashion industry); the term was originally associated with the secret language used by thieves and professional beggars. 'Argot' refers to the slang of a group that feels threatened by society, again, traditionally associated with criminals or thieves. 'Jargon' refers to the technical or highly specialized language of a professional group and is often unintelligible to outsiders.

25 **sound and sense:** For the idea of a direct relationship between sound and meaning, see the part on sound symbolism in Introduction, pp. li–lix.

26 **The faculty for making visible marks ... doubtless allied in many ways to drawing:** Tolkien himself partook in both activities, that he sees here as related to linguistic invention. His numerous alphabets and writing systems, as well as his talent for drawing and sketching, were an inherent part of his mythopoeia, as exemplified by *The Hobbit* and *The Lord of the Rings*. Many posthumous publications have revealed the wealth and breadth of Tolkien's activity in both of these spheres (e.g. *Artist*; Smith 2014).

27 **The faculty ... to drawing:** Between this paragraph and the next Tolkien has jotted down in pencil the phrase 'learnt alphabets' which seems to summarize the content of the preceding paragraph.

28 **The faculty for making visible marks ... now define:** In these two sections Tolkien uses parallelism to talk about a) the interconnectedness of learning to write and the visual arts; and b) the link between learning a language and using/appreciating

language as art. Note the repetition of the words 'faculty', 'latent', 'at least', 'practical object', 'highly developed', 'may lead to' and 'allied to'.

29 **An art for which life is not long enough:** Tolkien continued to work on his invented languages until his death in 1973, constantly amending and developing them.

30 **the construction of imaginary languages ... any critic that might occur:** The 'secret vice' Tolkien has been hinting at throughout the talk until this point, is here revealed in a concise definition. *Amusement*, for Tolkien, is a central objective of language-invention and stems from what he seems to see as a 'latent' human faculty to use language creatively as art or entertainment.

31 **of philologists:** These two words have been inserted after writing this line. This is one of only three pieces of evidence that there may have been a second delivery (or preparation for delivery) for 'A Secret Vice'; see Introduction, pp. xxxiii–xxxiv.

32 **'language' has more than one aspect, which may be specially developed:** On the left margin of the page, level with this sentence, Tolkien has added the word 'philosophic' in pencil. He may have been thinking about the philosophical languages of the seventeenth and eighteenth centuries, which aspired to a logical structure that would allow clarity of thought (see Introduction, pp. xlii–xliii).

33 **the other (notably not the originator) dropped off and became interested in drawing and design:** Marjorie Incledon; see note 18.

34 **Nevbosh, or the 'New Nonsense':** 'Nev' suggests 'new' while 'bosh' comes from Turkish in which it means literally 'empty.' 'Bosh' was popularised by the author J.J. Morier (1780–1849) in the 1834 novel *Ayesha: The Maid of Kars* to refer to 'nothing' (pp. 9, 20). Closer to Tolkien's time, it appears in the English poet and illustrator Edward Lear's made-up newspaper *The Nonsense Gazette* which talks of a Professor Bosh whose 'labours in the field of culinary and botanical science are so well known to all

the world' (Lear 2002, p. 240). Interestingly, Otto Jespersen notes the sound-symbolic quality of this word, listing it as one of the examples in words ending in a back vowel and /ʃ/ or /tʃ/ that are 'symbolic expressions for dislike, disgust, or scorn' (e.g. trash, tosh). He comments: 'E.[nglish] *bosh* (nonsense) is said to be a Turkish loan-word; it has become popular for the same reason for which the French nickname *boche* for a German was widely used during the [First] World War' (1922, pp. 401–2).

35 **I was older in secret vice:** This comment indicates that Tolkien was experimenting with language invention before Nevbosh, but there is no other evidence.

36 **Busbecq recorded for Crimean Gothic:** Ogier Ghiselin de Busbecq (1522–c.1592) was a Flemish diplomat and polymath who recorded the only surviving words of Crimean Gothic, a descendant of the Gothic language still spoken in an isolated area of the Crimea in the sixteenth century. Tolkien would attempt to invent a language influenced by Gothic in c.1911–12, called Gautisk (Smith 2006, pp. 274–7), and would make a similar effort in the 1930s with Taliska (Hostetter 2007b, pp. 341–2).

37 **almost 40:** This is the second of only three pieces of evidence that there may have been a second delivery (or preparation for delivery) for 'A Secret Vice'; see Introduction, pp. xxxiii–xxxiv.

38 **Dar fys ma vel gom co palt "hoc:** Humphrey Carpenter has translated this verse as follows:

> There was an old man who said 'How
> Can I possibly carry my cow?
> For if I were to ask it
> To get in my basket
> It would make such a terrible row!'
> (*Biography*, p. 36)

This fragment of *Nevbosh* is in a limerick form (5 lines, AABBA rhyming scheme, anapaestic metre). Edward Lear is known as one of the first Victorian poets to use this limerick form which had its origins in oral tradition (Lear 2002, p. 9). Lear may have chosen the limerick form as his poetic structure because it allowed for creative play and word rhyming. Prickett suggests that Lear used the limerick to invent his own nonsense world with talking animals, mysterious places and imaginary flora and fauna and contextualizes this with the Victorians' use of fantasy to create other worlds in order to escape from their own (2005, p. 109). The opening and subject of Tolkien's *Nevbosh* limerick also echoes one that Lear includes in the 1861 revised edition of *The Book of Nonsense* which mentions an old man and a troublesome cow:

> There was an Old Man who said, How
> Shall I flee from this horrible Cow?
> I will sit on the stile, and continue to smile
> Which may soften the heart of that Cow.
> (Lear 2002, p. 171)

39 **learned:** This is the third of only three pieces of evidence that there may have been a second delivery (or preparation for delivery) for 'A Secret Vice'; see Introduction, pp. xxxiii–xxxiv.

40 **This 'invention' is probably always going on . . . creation once for all in a distant past:** The idea that phonetic symbolism continues to be influential in language change (and not only in primordial times, at the beginning of language) is explored further in Tolkien's 'Essay on Phonetic' Symbolism; see p. 68.

41 **'phonetic predilection' – artistic phonetic expression:** A concise definition of a term that Tolkien explores more fully in his 'Essay on Phonetic Symbolism'.

42 **my inability to feel greatly wounded by m/n assonances in a rhyming poem:** Tolkien himself used such assonances in rhyming; e.g. in 'Errantry' he includes the lines:

> with elven knights of Aerie
> and Faerie, with *paladins*

that golden-haired, and shining-eyed
came riding by and *challenged him.*
(*Bombadil*, p. 59, emphasis added)

The rhyming 'paladins/challenged him' accepts the assonance of /n/ and /m/.

43 **roc/'rogo' ask; go/'ego' I; vel ('vieil, vieux' old); gom/'homo'
man:** *Rogo* and *ego* are Latin for 'ask' and 'I' respectively; *vieil*
and *vieux* are both masculine forms of the adjective for 'old' in
French (*vieil* is used in front of masculine nouns beginning with
a vowel or silent *h*; *vieux* is used in front of masculine nouns
beginning with a consonant).

44 **the ancient Germanic languages did not contribute:** Tolkien
here indicates that, although Nevbosh 'gom' may suggest the
Old English word for man, *guma*, this was by chance rather than
design.

45 **vacca, vache:** *Vacca* and *vache* are Latin and French respectively
for 'cow'.

46 **lint:** Tolkien would mark his pleasure with the sound aesthetic of
this invented word by carrying it through into his later language
invention. In his lexicon for the Gnomish language, developed
c.1917, there is an entry for the word *lint* (translated as 'quick,
nimble, light') and an indication that this word was the basis of
one of the early names for the great Elf leader and father of the
Elf princess Tinúviel (later Lúthien Tinúviel), Tinwë Linto
(Thingol in the published *Silmarillion*) (*PE* 11, p. 54). Later this
becomes in Quenya *linte*, as in the Quenya poem *Namárië*: 'Yéni
ve *lintë* yuldar avánier' ('Have passed like *swift* draughts').
Tolkien may have also used it later, in the name of his mysterious
creatures called 'lintips' in his 1965 poem 'Once upon a Time',
featuring Tom Bombadil (*Bombadil*, p. 280–2).

47 **Certainly, just as in real languages ... not by the relation of
sound and sense:** This is an idea further elaborated in Tolkien's
'Essay on Phonetic Symbolism'.

48 **We see it in an alloyed form in the peculiar keenness . . . long after they have become reasonably familiar with it:** Here Tolkien seems to be making a (rather cryptic) autobiographical allusion. In a 1955 letter to W.H. Auden, Tolkien famously described his reaction to the poetry of the *Kalevala* when he read it for the first time in the Finnish original with a metaphor: 'It was like discovering a complete wine-cellar filled with bottles of an amazing wine of a kind and flavour never tasted before. It quite intoxicated me' (*Letters*, pp. 213–14). His response to the lines 'Éala Éarendel engla beorhtost/ofer middangeard monnum sended!' ('Hail Earendel, brightest of angels, above the middle-earth sent unto men!') from the Old English poem *Christ*, which famously led to the adoption and adaptation of Earendel (later Eärendil) in Tolkien's mythology, is recorded via Arundel Lowdham, a character in Tolkien's unfinished *The Notion Club Papers*: 'When I came across that citation in the dictionary I felt a curious thrill, as if something had stirred in me, half wakened from sleep. There was something very remote and strange and beautiful behind those words, if I could grasp it, far beyond ancient English' (*Sauron Defeated*, p. 236).

49 **I have heard others independently voice my own feeling that the Welsh names . . . the barest knowledge of Welsh spelling sufficient for them to cease to be jumbles of letters:** In a January 1965 radio interview with Denys Gueroult Tolkien replied to a question about what languages most helped him in the writing of *The Lord of the Rings* with 'I should have said Welsh has always attracted me by its style and sound more than any other, even though I first only saw it on coal-trucks. I always wanted to know what it was about' (*BBC Interview*, p. 5). In his O'Donnell lecture on 'English and Welsh' Tolkien noted that the Welsh language first 'struck' him 'in the names on coal-trucks' and the hint of 'a language old and yet alive . . . pierced my linguistic heart' (*Monsters*, p. 192). In the same lecture he declared: 'Welsh is beautiful' and that his appreciation of the sounds of Welsh was

not 'peculiar to myself among the English. It is not. It is present in many of them. It lies dormant, I believe, in many more of those who today live in Lloegr [England] and speak Saesneg [English]' (*Monsters*, pp. 189, 194).

50 **the resplendent 'lost Gothic' poetry, may still be recaptured:** In c.1908–9, Tolkien's study of Germanic myth and legend led him to discover the remains of the oldest known Germanic language, Gothic, through Joseph Wright's 1899 *Primer of the Gothic Language*. In this primer, Wright not only outlined the Gothic language but also included a series of introductory chapters which reconstructed the Proto-Germanic vowel and consonant sound systems that resulted in Gothic. It is only after that introductory matter that Wright launches into the grammar and syntax of the actual Gothic language. As Tolkien later recounted of this primer, 'I discovered in it not only modern historical philology, which appealed to the historical and scientific side, but for the first time the study of a language out of mere love' (*Letters*, p. 213). The Gothic language was intriguing to Tolkien for two reasons. First, because of its tantalizingly small vocabulary based on the few extant Gothic texts; and secondly due to the potential for (re)constructing lost words based on the phonetic and syntactical rules outlined in the Wright grammar. Indeed, for Tolkien the Goths represented a lost culture and held the potential to build upon the corpora of words and texts to reconstruct lost names and tales. Tolkien would attempt to invent a hypothetical Germanic language from which Gothic supposedly emerged, Gautisk, which also would have been the language of the Geats, the people of *Beowulf*. He would use the same notebook he would later use to start work on his Qenya language in early 1915 (see Smith 2006, pp. 272–4).

51 **meccano:** A model construction set created in Liverpool by Frank Hornby in 1901.

52 **a very alien word-form could be constructed out of purely English phonetic elements ... scratch becomes štærks, each**

'phoneme' being perfectly native, the total entirely foreign: Tolkien's idea here of creating 'alien'-sounding words by turning them backwards phonetically has an interesting parallel in 'On Fairy-stories'. In the section on 'Recovery, Escape, Consolation' Tolkien argues for the restorative quality of fantasy, because it allows us to see the mundane world afresh. He mentions *Mooreeffoc*, or Chestertonian Fantasy, as an example of the 'freshness of vision' that fantasy can offer:

> *Mooreeffoc* is a fantastic word, but it could be seen written up in every town in this land. It is Coffee-room, viewed from the inside through a glass door, as it was seen by Dickens on a dark London day; and it was used by Chesterton to denote the queerness of things that have become trite, when they are seen suddenly from a new angle. (*TOFS*, p. 68)

Tolkien's example of a trite native English word turned 'alien', and acquiring a sense of 'individuality', links the creativity and artistic qualities of language invention with the 'recovery' of fantasy. Tolkien also mentions *štærks*/scratch in his 'Essay on Phonetic Symbolism' (see p. 71) at a point where he explores the 'phonetic predilections' of specific languages. The significance of these words only becomes apparent in this essay.

53 **very possibly cutá – ever is certainly part of vrú and cedo, cesso of cutár:** Tolkien is here indicating that the Naffarin words *cutá* and *vrú* were influenced by the Latin verbs 'cedo' and 'cesso', and by the English word 'ever', respectively. *Cedo* means (verb) 'go, move along' and *cesso* means (verb) 'delay, rest, be free of'.

54 **vrú 'ever' . . . is the only word of interest from this point of view:** The persistence of this word form in Tolkien's later language invention can be seen in the *Qenya Lexicon* where it appears as the root VORO 'ever, always' (*PE* 12, p. 102). From this root Tolkien would construct the name of the first wife and then faithful companion of Eärendil the Mariner, *Voronwë* (p. 102). In the 1930s *Etymologies*, Tolkien would cite the Qenya

form *voro* ('ever, continually') and through such invented words as *voro-gandele* 'harping on one tune' link it with the idea of 'continual repetition' (*Lost Road*, p. 353). Tolkien would also develop a Noldorin root BORÓN- from which he constructed Old Noldorin words such as *bronie*, 'last, endure, lasting', and *brūna*, 'that has long endured, old (only used of things, and implies that they are old, but not changed or worn out' (ibid.). This form is also found in the name of Boromir which is 'an old Noldorin name of ancient origin also borne by Gnomes' (ibid.). The name means 'steadfast jewel' which, taking into account Boromir's actions in *The Lord of the Rings*, gives it a certain irony.

55 **I recently became possessed by accident of some secret documents:** Tolkien is here using the 'found manuscript' topos that works such as Percy Greg's *Across the Zodiac* used to introduce invented languages. Tolkien used this conceit a number of times in his creative writing, including in *The Notion Club Papers* (supposedly papers found within waste paper by the Clerk of the Examination Schools at Oxford, and which were subsequently edited by him; see *Sauron Defeated*, p. 155) and, of course, in *The Lord of the Rings*, in the Prologue of which Tolkien claims that: 'This account of the end of the Third Age is drawn mainly from the Red Book of Westmarch' which he 'translated' (*Fellowship*, p. 14; *Return*, p. 1133–8).

56 **in the Fonwegian language spoken apparently in the island of Fonway:** There are no notes on these pages about the etymology of the names Fonway or Fonwegian and Tolkien's invented lexicons do not include any roots or words that may shed light on this. However, a very early rebus message that Tolkien composed for his guardian at that time, Father Francis Morgan, contains the phrase '"cheefongy" dances', the meaning of which may be 'cheap French dances' (see Higgins 2015, p. 58). If that suggestion is correct, then the name of this language may be associated with French, a language that Tolkien notes as an inspiration, in part, for the grammar of Fonwegian. The fact that Fonway is an island,

and that further down Tolkien makes a comparison of Fonwegian with Jonathan Swift's languages in *Gulliver's Travels*, may give credence to the hypothesis that the entire interlude of Fonwegian is an intertextual play on *Gulliver's Travels*, itself a story of travel in exotic islands where strange tongues are spoken. Fonway also brings to mind the island of Formosa (modern-day Taiwan) and the specimens of the Formosan language published by George Psalmanazar, a friend of Samuel Johnson. The Formosan language became an eighteenth-century sensation, but was eventually proved to be a fabrication (see Conley and Cain 2006, pp. 85–6).

57 **but os neuter always next stem is carried out through all the forms:** Tolkien seems to be pointing out an anomaly with the neutral gender in his declension of the Fonwegian personal pronoun. In Fonwegian, gender, number and cases are indicated by suffixes (the masculine seems to be the root, to which one can add -e for feminine, -os for neutral, -er for plural and -is for the genitive case). The regular order of suffixes seems to be: root + number + case + gender, so, for example, in the declension of 'con' below, *conerise* is feminine plural in the genitive (con + -er for plural + -is for genitive + -e for feminine). However, this rule does not hold for the neuter, in which the suffix for gender is always the first one to be added to the root. So Tolkien gives *wonoser* for neutral plural (won + -os for neutral + -er for plural), which according to the rule above should have been *woneros* (won + -er for plural + -os for neutral).

58 **The 'agglutinative' idea:** Refers to those languages in which words and grammatical forms are created by adding elements (e.g. prefixes, infixes, and suffixes) to a root without any morphological change to the root or the added elements. The term was introduced by the German philosopher Wilhelm von Humboldt (1767–1835) and is derived from the Latin verb *agglutinare*, to glue together.

59 **The whole is slightly reminiscent in fact of 'the Swiftian'**

characters as seen in Scraps vouchsafed of the Lilliputian, Blefuscudian, and Brobdingnagian idioms: In *Gulliver's Travels* (1726), a parody of the 'traveller's tale' genre, Jonathan Swift used language invention, fuelled by political satire, to create place-names and sample phrases and fragments in several imaginative languages. One of the key distinguishing elements of Swift's language invention was their sound-aesthetic construction, which aimed to distinguish the nature and culture of the different races that Swift's ship surgeon, Lemuel Gulliver, encountered on his fantastical travels (see also Introduction, xli). Tolkien studied Swift's invention of names and fragments of languages for the islands Gulliver explored and made a list of them as part of his notes for 'A Secret Vice'; see 'The Manuscripts', pp. 86–7.

60 **We may leave out his horse language:** Swift's invented language for the *Houyhnhnms*, a race of civilized horses who lived on an island with the barbarous *Yahoos*. For the *Houyhnhnms*, Swift invented words that use onomatopoeia that makes them sound like a horse's whinny. For example the invented word in *Houyhnhnm* for 'bird of prey' is *Gnnayh* (Swift 2005, p. 231).

61 **largely an eye joke (and not very good):** The point Tolkien may be making here is that the language of the Houyhnhnms is largely unpronounceable and can only be appreciated when seen on the page, something which defeats the purpose of onomatopoeia.

62 **but skill need not be expended solely on canvases of 80 square feet; there are smaller experiments and sketches:** Tolkien's metaphor for constructing an entire invented language (an enormous canvas) vs. jotting down just one intriguing element of such a language (smaller experiments and sketches) brings to mind a similar metaphor of the 'large canvas' and the 'single leaf' in his short story 'Leaf by Niggle', composed in 1938–9 and first published in *The Dublin Review* in 1945. In this story the artist Niggle is painting a canvas of a giant tree with a forest in the distance. In doing this, he focuses on every single leaf of the tree with an

obsessive attention to detail. It has been argued that Tolkien is allegorically referring here to his own creative process (see Shippey 2000, pp. 266–77). He wanted to finish the 'big tree', i.e. the grand-narrative of his mythology, but often 'niggled' with minute details of one particular tale.

63 **the making of language and mythology are related functions . . . by-product to main manufacture):** One of the key foundational statements in Tolkien's creative and mythic process. He would revisit this idea in his 'On Fairy-stories': 'Mythology is language and language is mythology. The mind, and the tongue, and the tale are coeval' (*TOFS*, p. 181; see also Introduction, pp. xi–xiii).

64 **individual linguistic character:** Tolkien would explore this concept more fully in his October 1955 talk 'English and Welsh' which was the inaugural of the O'Donnell Lectures. The lecture was first published in the volume *Angles and Britons: O'Donnell Lectures* (1963) and then in 1983 it was reprinted in *The Monsters and the Critics and Other Essays* (pp. 162–97). In this talk, Tolkien suggested that everyone has their own personal 'linguistic potential': 'we each have a *native language*. But that is not the language that we speak, our cradle-tongue, the first-learned . . . My chief point here is to emphasize the difference between the first-learned language, the language of custom, and an individual's native language, his inherent linguistic predilections' (*Monsters*, p. 190). For a discussion of Tolkien's theory of 'inherent linguistic predilections' see Fimi 2008, pp. 80–3.

65 **There is the grammatical and logical . . . consider the categories and the relations of words, and the various neat, effective, or ingenious ways in which these can be expressed:** This point brings to mind the pursuit for philosophical universal languages in the seventeenth and eighteenth centuries, which invented words from scratch based on a complex system of how notions and objects are interrelated. See Introduction, pp. xlii–xliii.

66 **those many unnamed geniuses who have invented the skilful**

bits of machinery in our traditional languages: Tolkien's idea that *individuals* can contribute to language change is somewhat idiosyncratic. He touches upon this notion in his 'Essay on Phonetic Symbolism' (see p. 71) but he explores it much further in his creative writing. In Tolkien's mythology, the Elves – especially the Noldor – are the ultimate linguists: they create ideal languages, capable of aesthetic beauty and sound symbolism. Tolkien writes that:

> the tongue of the Noldor had changed for the most part only in the making of new words (for things new and old), and in *the wilful altering* of the ancient tongue of the Quendi *to forms and patterns that seemed to the Eldar more beautiful*. (*Jewels*, p. 28, emphasis added)

In another instance it is claimed that:

> They [the Noldor] were changeful in speech, for they had great love of words, and sought ever *to find names more fit* for all things that they knew or imagined. (*Lost Road*, 223, emphasis added)

The Elves, therefore, become the primary agents of linguistic creativity in Middle-earth and the beauty of their languages is attributed to their artistic nature. See also Fimi 2008, pp. 93–115.

67 **The beautiful phonologies . . . will not interest you:** By the time Tolkien first gave this talk in 1931 he had been working on his Elvish language invention since early 1915 and had amassed a large collection of phonologies, grammars and word lists for the various stages of his system of Elvish languages. The great majority of this work did not see publication until after Tolkien's death.

68 **my own most normal phonetic taste:** Tolkien refers here to his love and appreciation of Finnish. For his discovery and enthusiasm for Finnish, see Introduction, pp. xvii and Kahlas-Tarkka 2014.

69 **one has moods in this as in all other matters of taste:** Tolkien makes a very similar point in a 1955 letter to W.H. Auden:

Linguistic taste changes like everything else, as time goes on; or oscillates between poles. Latin and the British type of Celtic have it now, with the beautifully co-ordinated and patterned (if simply patterned) Anglo-Saxon near at hand and further off the Old Norse with the neighbouring but alien Finnish. Roman-British might not one say? With a strong but more recent infusion from Scandinavia and the Baltic. Well, I daresay such linguistic tastes, with due allowance for school-overlay, are as good or better a test of ancestry as blood-groups. (*Letters*, p. 214)

70 **A consequent weakness . . . blood or the heat of the world such as critics demand:** Writers of the early twentieth century consciously saw themselves as breaking away from the sentimentality and often florid style of Victorian literature, exemplified by Gertrude Stein's call to 'kill the nineteenth century' and Ezra Pound's motto 'make it new'. On the contrary, a lot of Tolkien's work fits better with the Victorian and Edwardian milieu he was brought up in (see Fimi 2008).

71 **Oilima Markirya:** Tolkien composed twelve versions of this Qenya poem which were variously titled *Oilima Markirya* or 'The Last Ship' or 'The Last Ark'. All twelve versions have been published with notes and commentary in *Parma Eldalamberon* 16, pp. 53–87. Three of these versions appear in this volume. This is the first one, which Tolkien incorporated in the 'Secret Vice' paper itself. The other two variant versions are included in 'The Manuscripts' (pp. 89–90, 102–4). The melancholy image of a white ship departing suggests similar imagery with the end of *The Lord of the Rings*: 'and the sails were drawn up, and the wind blew, and slowly the ship slipped away down the long grey firth' (*Return*, p. 1030).

72 **Oilima Markirya:** This is a typed page, and the title of the poem is hand-written at the top.

73 **The ~~Last Ship~~ Ark:** The translation of the poem's title in this typescript appears as 'The Last Ship' but Tolkien has crossed out 'Ship' and handwritten 'Ark'.

74 **bleared:** This word is circled in pencil

75 **Nieninqe:** The title of this poem can be found in *The Qenya Lexicon*, under the root NYEHE, 'weep', from which 'nieninqe' means 'snowdrop', but literally 'white tear' (*PE* 12, p. 68).

76 **Nielikkilis:** The name of the character who is the subject of this poem is also given in *The Qenya Lexicon*: 'Nieliqi also Nielikki or Nyelikki' (*PE* 12, p. 68; Tolkien here uses the second form, but in the diminutive). Tolkien glosses this name as 'a little girl among the Valar who danced in the spring – where her tears fell snow-drops sprang, where her feet touched as she danced daffodils blossomed' (ibid., pp. 68–9). Higgins (2015) suggests that in *The Book of Lost Tales* Nieninqe may have originally been one of the mortal children who trod the Olorë Mallë, the pathway of dreams, and sadly did not return; presumably causing her, her parents, or both to weep.

77 **Earendel:** One of two versions of this poem in this volume. The original form of this name was 'Earendl' and it is found in *The Qenya Lexicon* glossed as 'the wanderer, the greater sailor who sailed up into the sky in his ship Vingelot, which now is the morning or evening star' (*PE* 12, p. 34). By the time of this poem, Earendel had become an important character in Tolkien's mythology as the mariner who sailed West in search of his father and after many marvellous adventures came to Valinor, the land of the Gods. In later versions of the mythology, Tolkien changed the motivation for Earendel's sailing West: instead of an adven-turer he became an emissary of Men and Elves to the Valar, asking them to intervene and defeat the evil that had enthralled Middle-earth.

78 **Earendel at the Helm:** The page that contains this 'poetic' trans-lation, as opposed to the 'prose' translation that precedes it, is a typescript, consecutively numbered with the previous and following handwritten pages.

79 **a totally different if related language:** This poem fragment is written in Noldorin, a language Tolkien developed from his

earlier Gnomish or Goldogrin (c.1917–20) which he had devised
during the writing of the 'Book of Lost Tales' and was influenced
by Welsh. Later, when Tolkien was composing the Appendices of
The Lord of the Rings he revised the fictional history of this lan-
guage and renamed it Sindarin. See Introduction, p. xxviii.

80 **Tumledin/the Smooth Valley:** Tolkien is setting the action of
this poem in the mountains overlooking Tumledin which is a
variant name of 'Tumladin', the Valley of Smoothness. This
name first appears in 'The Fall of Gondolin' in *The Book of Lost
Tales* to describe the plain or vale of Gondolin (*Lost Tales II*, pp.
163–4; 167–8). The two elements of the place-name are found in
The Gnomish Lexicon: *tûm*, 'valley' (*PE* 11, p. 71) and *ladin*, 'level,
smooth' (ibid., p. 52). When Gnomish was re-conceived as
Noldorin, *ladin* became Noldorin *lhaden* (pl. *lhedin*) meaning
'flat, smooth' (*PE* 13, p. 148). Although the name appears as
'Tumladin' throughout Tolkien's mythology, here he is evidently
experimenting with the form 'Tumledin'. In *The Etymologies*,
written after delivering 'A Secret Vice', Tolkien would slightly
modify the derivation of this name again by inventing the root
LAT-, 'lie open', giving the Noldorin word 'lhaden', and chang-
ing the gloss of 'Tumladen' to the 'plain of Gondolin' (*Lost Road*,
p. 368).

81 **Nebrachar:** In the first edition of 'A Secret Vice' Christopher
Tolkien noted that: 'the name *Nebrachar* occurs nowhere else,
and whatever story may be glimpsed in this poem cannot be
identified in any form of the mythology that is extant' (*Monsters*,
p. 220). Although many posthumous publications of Tolkien's
work have appeared since then, this name is still not attested.
However, in the 'Early Noldorin Fragments' there are two roots:
NEB, 'near' (*PE* 13, p. 164), and RHACH, 'carnage, slaughter'
(ibid., p. 152), so Nebrachar may mean 'near a place of slaughter'.

82 **Yrch/Stonefaces:** *Yrch* is the Noldorin plural form of *orch* 'orc,
goblin' (*PE* 13, p. 151). Tolkien's translation of this word as
'Stonefaces' is interesting and unique. Tolkien's earliest conception

of orcs (which would go through many changes as he developed his mythology) included imagery of stones and rocks when he described them as made by Melkor from 'subterranean heats and slime. Their hearts were of granite and their bodies deformed; foul their faces which smiled not' (*Lost Tales II*, pp. 159–60).

83 **Damrod/Damrod (a hunter):** One of the youngest of the seven sons of the Noldorin Elf and artificer Fëanor, maker of the three Silmarils from the last light of the two trees of Valinor. Damrod is known as a great hunter (*Shaping*, p. 15). Like his brothers, Damrod is bound by oath to recover the Silmarils from the evil Morgoth who stole them with the help of the spider Ungoliant. Damrod is mentioned in *The Lay of Leithian* (*Lays*, p. 211) and appears many times in *The Sketch of the Mythology* and the 1930s *Quenta Silmarillion*.

84 **Luithien/Lúthien:** The name of the Elvish princess Lúthien Tinuviel in Tolkien's *The Gest of Beren and Lúthien* (*Lays*, p. 153) which is one of the great story-cycles of Tolkien's legendarium.

85 **Eglavar/Elfland:** This appears to be a unique form of Noldorin Eglamar which is cognate with the Qenya place name Eldamar, meaning 'Elf land'. Egla appears in the *Gnomish Lexicon* as a 'name of the fairies given by the *Gwalin* [the Valar], and adopted largely by them' (*PE* 11, p. 32). The 'var' element of Eglavar suggests a variant form of the Qenya root MBARA ('land, dwelling') which has a Gnomish cognate -*bar* (*PE* 12, p. 60). According to the *Early Noldorin Grammar* the phoneme /b/ may mutate to either /bh/ or /v/ (*PE* 13, p. 120), which may explain the variant form Eglavar (from Eglamar).

86 **in the Kalevala . . . mere notes in a phonetic tune struck to harmonize with penkerelle, or tuimenia which do 'mean' something:** Tolkien is quoting nearly verbatim from C.N.E. Eliot's *A Finnish Grammar* (1890), from his description of the dialect of the *Kalevala* (pp. 228–9). Eliot's *Grammar*, which includes reading selections from the *Kalevala* runos in the back of the book, would be the first Tolkien would use in his attempt

as an undergraduate at Oxford to learn Finnish. Eliot notes that there is in the *Kalevala*:

> a habit of repeating the same idea under numerous synonyms for the sake of emphasis and of creating new words for the sake of parallelism or alliteration, which have sometimes a meaning and bear testimony to the flexibility and fecundity of the language, but sometimes are absolutely unmeaning. Thus in Kal. xi. 55 we have Enkä lähe Inkerelle, Penkerelle, pänkerelle. Here pänkerelle means nothing at all, but is simply a kind of repetition of penkerelle. Similarly Kal. xlviii. 100, Ihveniä, ahvenia, Tuimenia, taimenia. Ihveniä and Tuimenia are meaningless words. (pp. 228–9)

Tolkien has got *taimenia* and *tuimenia* confused here, as he claims that the former is 'non-significant' and the latter has a meaning, while Eliot clearly states that it is *tuimenia* that is a 'meaningless word'. Leena Kahlas-Tarkka has hypothesized that this error in the published 'A Secret Vice' in *The Monsters and the Critics* may be due to 'an editorial slip' (2014, p. 270), but the manuscript shows that this is Tolkien's genuine error instead. It must have been a temporary slip for Tolkien, though, as he uses the same argument and same examples about the Finnish language in his *Kalevala* essay, and in that case he is right about the 'meaningless' words: 'pänkerelle merely echoes Penkerelle, and Ihveniä and Tuimenia are merely invented to set off ahvenia and taimenia' (*Kullervo*, p. 77).

87 **invention of the free adjective ... pictures in the mind:** Here Tolkien anticipates some of the ideas he would develop later in 'On Fairy-stories', about the power of language and the way it affects not only our perception of the world but also our imagination. Tolkien also uses the coinage 'green sun' in 'On Fairy-stories' (*TOFS*, p. 61).

PART II

'Essay on Phonetic Symbolism'

This essay (MS Tolkien 24, folios 3–7 and 9) was written in blue ink on eight leaves of 'Oxford paper' torn out from examination booklets and then folded in the middle to form a mini-booklet of half the dimensions of the original. Although it is impossible to be certain, it appears as though the essay was written in one sitting: the same ink is used throughout, and all emendations look contemporary.

Although there are a number of themes and ideas that this essay shares with 'A Secret Vice', its main topic is different and it is ostensibly an independent work by Tolkien. It may be that his first idea for a paper for the Johnson Society was on the topic of phonetic symbolism, which he later abandoned, choosing instead the more self-reflective and personal subject of language invention. Another possibility is that Tolkien stopped in the middle of composing 'A Secret Vice' and began writing this separate essay to address some of the ideas that were related to, but not central in, his paper. In our notes we cross-reference shared ideas between the two essays, so that the reader can easily see how Tolkien briefly sketched main concepts in one essay that he then explored more fully in the other.

Phonetic Symbolism[1]: What is meant? I don't know. What do I mean? That may appear connected with two things which are not the same – i.e. are clearly not (wholly symbolic):

(a) onomatopoeia[2] (b) national and individual phonetic predilection (of which more later). Onomatopoeia is not in essence 'symbolic'. In essence or rather in rudest form it means imitating physical sounds with organs of speech (sometimes and by some persons this can be accomplished with a very great acoustic verisimilitude). But 'phonetic symbolism' cannot be discussed without allusion to onomatopoeia. If a 'symbolic' feeling really exists it must largely owe its origin to the refinement ~~and~~ of onomatopoeia. Also an element that is not mere imitation but is 'symbolic' comes in this: (a) the ~~sound-imit~~ noise-imitation becomes a word for something that is not only a noise, though it is associated with one (wind, merriment, ~~dr~~ waterfall, cow)

(b) 'phonetic predilection' comes in, and the 'imitation-noise' is a mere sketch or suggestion of the original, and its phonetic form is made to conform to this phonetic predilection of the language. The onomatopoeia is thus again removed a stage further from its purely 'echoic' basis, and can become one of the sources of a 'linguistic feeling' – a readiness to associate notions with sound-groups (to make words). Thus a language not possessing b cannot imitate in the language (apart from the individual efforts of an animal imitator) the cry of sheep as baa.

I will use Phonetic Symbolism therefore to mean the idea or belief or fact that certain combinations of sounds are more fitted to express certain notions than to express others: that certain groups of notions tend to be expressed (in all languages, or widely among languages) by ~~words~~ sound groups having certain phonetic elements. This specially in {the} case where onomatopoeia is not present, or is no longer obvious.

Thus (a) that SEK is 'more suitable' to express 'cut' than, say MU, MUL etc. [This is usually more convincing negatively].

(b) a word for 'little', or diminutive suffixes, are specially associated with vowel i, ī[3] (pretty for pratty[4], teeny for tiny, little – but small, minute tiny, and 'micel'[5].)

Now the belief in this – even if it does not delve lower & seek to explore the reasons for such a 'sense of fitness' – encounters difficulties as soon as we come to discuss actual cases.

First of all: do you mean common human taste or instinct – something which will perhaps remain when all sorts of local and racial differences are deducted – such as in another sphere of taste and symbolism make an African's choice of colours (either to express 'predilection' as in his clothes or furnishings, or a 'symbolism' to express mourning) different from an Englishman's. Something like 'black'. (Is black disliked because of night, or be night because it is black)?

But this would requires a painful analysis of many languages – and it is as we shall see, even this would yield results of dubious value (because language has a history). Accident? katkaise[6] (Finnish): English cut.

In any case (as I have suggested by the word negative above) even if you select a 'notion' which is obviously most likely to be favourable (i.e. susceptible liable to be expressed in sounds having a 'symbolic' value, if any notion ever is) – such as 'cut'. There remains a wide neutral area. You cannot predict what form the word will take in any given language – and this is probably not due only to these cases (though it is this may constitute) – to history and inheritance with its accidents. Not even if you know something of the phonetic predilection of the language, or words for 'cut' in hundreds of others. This is due probably to 'margin' – the farther you get from obvious onomatopoeia. Semantic Shift eg. Welsh torri break – also cut in use torri barf[7], trancher[8], τέμνω (τμη, τομ)[9] snip (*sneit), cut, seco[10], torri (naddu[11])

You may expect – or may say that you yourself prefer the presence of a voiceless stop (especially k) in your sound-group, and the concomitance of a hiss sound (s, š, tš) or perhaps a t. But you don't necessarily get it. You would not expect mu – and you probably won't get it. – there is perhaps food for thought in that.

The most serious problem of all is provided by the fact that 'language' is obviously now very old – the one instrument that is common to the race. Even if you assume (and it is an assumption because no recording philologist was present at the birth of language or of any language other than 'artificial international languages' which {are} only a special product of the natural, as a pollard willow is to a wild tree) that this "symbolism" played a part in the invention and making current of linguistic material – it is clear that this sort of 'artistry' (as we may call it) soon evaporates, and the notion or value dominates.[12] A gold currency of 'real' value is quickly succeeded by tokens, or paper. Thus sound-groups associated with notions obviously capable of onomatopoetic ~~coinag~~ representation – sheep (baa-lamb), cow (moo-cow), waterfall (fors[13]), noise (hullabaloo, hubbub, din, boom, bang, clang, row) – soon came into existence which either do not have this origin, or no longer have this character: noise, hávaði[14]. The very development shows the ~~possibility of~~ waning of phonetic attention, or at least the possibility of this. cf. Gothic teiƕō 'thunder'

Most serious is the consideration that "inattentive phonetic change" – i.e. the sort that falls into "sound-laws" – probably affects the 'symbolic instinct' (or would if it existed) itself. Since the notional association goes on after shift in the sound-form. Much (if not all) of what people imagine to be the "phonetic fitness" of a sound-symbol (e.g. <u>seco</u>) is due probably (a) to familiarity – with the association – just as the English translation of the ~~Our~~ <u>pater noster</u> may be regarded as felicitous, and as the felicity of ancient verse in a language only known through its later remains, and not independently, is apt to be overestimated by its special students. (b) to a compound in the mind of the symbols associated with a notion in their own language or others known. This can be tested by getting people to try and invent words. Much of individual tasting remains dark (and there is pure caprice), but the 'known languages' usually come to expression[15]. So languages invent new words out of old – Germanic group <u>wōp</u> – <u>hrōp</u> – <u>hwōp</u> (hwōt).[16] The English <u>flash</u> group (lash, splash, plash, slash, dash, hash, rash) crash, clash, squash, mash, smash, bash.

It is clear, therefore, that ~~before we can~~ in order to get down to any basic <u>phonetic symbolism</u> valid (with variations) generally or widely – <u>living</u> on {in} even the <u>old recorded</u> languages of the world can only be used with great caution – and then probably without certain results.

Only certain classes of words are susceptible for study. Not only especially those that are held <u>poetic</u>. Probably the reason why they <u>are</u> (cf. Barfield[17]) – a link still felt between form and content. Many words are built out of notional counters taken at random as need altered, not "poetically" constructed. None can purely say what is phonetically symbolic a "fit" to represent "parasynthetic", or "philology", or "proportional representation". Many of the others have wandered <u>notionally</u> so far from the original (even when form has remained more or less static) that a long history has to be known before their evidence for this purpose can be valid – e.g. even in the case of relatively recent words like boast, a word of "obscure" origin appearing in the Middle Ages – with senses like uproar, noise, – and as Americans say 'big noise' so also glory, pride.

The failure to recognise this is what vitiates (or renders null) the work of enthusiasts working from a physical side chiefly like Paget[18] – they lack historical learning; they probably do not know sufficiently about the history of any one language; they take the words of modern recorded uncivilized languages[19] as if they were new creations in the void. In other words their work, as they perform it is useless. To what value (if any) comparisons of the "words" for the same notions over a vast slew of languages might have, I will return in a moment.

Personally, after a statement of all the difficulties (attending the valuation of the evidence) I may say that I believe there is such a thing as 'phonetic symbolism' as defined – though it becomes vague and less susceptible of analysis or demonstration the more general (the more means: human) you try to make it, i.e. the more means you try to free it from this accidental local colouring of inheritance with which it is always ultimately bound up. It is like trying to find pure water.

I think it exists and existed, and was once stronger – or rather in languages as the rational and analytic gradually gains upper hand (and the notion gets more separated from the symbol) it is weakened. But even say in English (a fairly extreme example of a largely desiccated language) it remains operative as a disturbing factor in the way of the smooth course of bold semantic and phonetic inheritance. It is principally seen as a disturbing factor in the parallel and synchronized development of meaning and form. It is an element not only in re-creation but in obsolescence and loss.

There is this justification for seeing "phonetic fitness" even in modern words: for instance a word may be known to the historical and lexicographical philologists to be a loan of such and such a date or an ancient inheritance. But he would have to know a word's real history (which includes its relation to (a) all words of similar meaning (b) all words of similar form – the 2 permanent lines of association) to say that its adoption or per-sistence was not due to a sense of fitness of form. ~~Then~~ But the 'fitness' is often not symbolic but mere convenience (root {illeg} wyrt wala)[20]; the 'fitness' is mostly a product of the association of all words of similar form and similar sound (which is apt to work at once on the meaning & forms of this diverse group)[21] rather than only mere ~~mystical or fe~~ mysteries – at least in the fully-fledged languages we know about.

The interference or the cause of phonetic inheritance may be observed in irregular forms taken by some words thunder (in which thunner is from oblique thúr- > thour)[22]: – this may only operate through choice among 'legitimate' versions. A guess case is muckle – mickle[23] in the proverb[24]. But this has also had fitness in the "local" influence of little. Possibly weak for wook, or woke.[25]

Another case is the shift of meaning with phonetic shift and presumably caused by it. (mickle)[26] This again is not necessarily to be denied because it consists in isolating, or making domi-nant, one sense ~~which~~ of several, which had risen semantically and independent of form. Cf. doom – how far is this due to Doomsday, how far to isolation of a meaning and colouration of it by form (gloom, loom, boom – but bloom, plume, fume). Doomsday cannot however in the last resort be deemed to be a more potent word than das jüngste Gericht[27] – for English ears.

Does it affect din (older *duni[28])? I think it does – but it is plain that inherited contexts still grip this word and prevent it thinning down by association with tin, thin, tinkle, ring. The

"phonetic symbolists" would say also the heavy d - but dig -
ding - dim).

As a footnote I would advert to the notion that "onomato-
poeia" resist 'sound-laws'. The notion {is} probably false. Resistance
does not occur when the words {are?} of such origin and become
real ~~noises~~ words. People for generations may make the same or
similar shouts at a crow's noise, but ~~a word~~ if this imitation
becomes the word's name it will shift – rook is no longer krāg or
krāk or χrāk from which it took its use[29]. Lallwörter[30] are a special
class – they are ?perpet[ually] resuscitated.

I have kept pretty close to onomatopoeia as the borderland.
More interesting would be cases, if we could find them, in which
"abstract" notions, or words not naturally associated with sounds
in the exterior world, were felt to have a natural or fit symbol.
Good, bad, blue, dark, come, go, see, feel, know & so on. I
leave this point open. But such experience as I have points to the
conclusion that either a 'sound notion' is present (~~the difficult~~ it
is in an astonishingly large number of the cases susceptible of
treatment) or else the fitness is due to known languages. Try
blue, or red karne – but elements in this are obvious [31].

Old writers (and some moderns) used to deal in the mystic
value of "letters". Here they say – on rather individual sounds
or phonemes. L? It gives me pleasure. Any language I invent
would abound in l. But some languages haven't got it (Old
Iranian. Japanese)

There is a related topic I will touch on in conclusion.
'Phonetic-predilection'. Phonetic-predilection is different from
mere caprice which is related rather to the ~~expa~~ exclamatory
noises which remain outside 'formal language' and even con-
tain words foreign to the latter, or so contrary to phonetic
predilection. Eg. humph m̃m̃ And the perversions of yes and
no. Phonetic predilection is rather that which determines the

forms of a given language – or the sum of the observed (or instinct appreciated) facts[32].

Thus – what makes Greek so Greek? In what lies the Greekness of Greek, the Welshness of Welsh, the Englishness of English? štærks/scratch.[33]

No grammar of, say, Gothic is really complete without an attempt to analyse, or at least point to some salient features in the Gothicness of Gothic, showing (a) what is Gothic in distinction to ~~all~~ all non-Gothic (b) what is shared, e.g. by old Germanic dialects (Old High German). This is particularly important in a language showing a clean and homogenous individuality. It distinguishes dialects. It is one of the explanations of the attractions of such languages – e.g. of the Germanic dialects; and of the pathetic fallacy scoffed at (but not explained) by Sweet in the preface to his dictionary[34]: to 'pure Saxon English'[35]. It is in the palate in every line of Homer. It gives the sound to Beowulf or Eddaic verse. It gives Esperanto a value exceeding that of other and technically better cultured (simpler) competitors.

The connexion of this with 'phonetic symbolism' is this – I believe they are connected. For though this 'system' is largely a product of inheritance I believe that the individual "phonetic predilection" is not necessarily (perhaps never quite) identical with that of this system[36]. [Less so in some educated communities when knowledge of other systems interferes]. That is distinct from though dominated by the inheritance there is in an individual instinct for word formation: "phonetic symbolism".

The divergence of the individual from system, probably a disturbing element, and one of the generators of "sound-change".[37] Where this divergence is common to many – as is liable to happen in those related by blood, associated by habit, locality etc.– this may come to effect; where they are isolated they perish.[38]

NOTES

1 **Phonetic Symbolism:** Various terms have been used to describe the direct relationship between the sounds making up a word and its meaning. Tolkien was familiar with Jespersen's use of 'sound symbolism' and Bloomfield's rejection of *Lautsymbolik*, but here he adopts the term preferred by Edward Sapir, whose 'Study in Phonetic Symbolism' had been published in 1929 (two years before Tolkien delivered 'A Secret Vice'). Sapir gave the subjects of his studies meaningless words asking them to associate them with size, finding that large size was assigned by most participants to words containing the vowel *a*, as opposed to those containing the vowel *i*, which were associated with small size. For a discussion of Tolkien's awareness of contemporary research on sound symbolism, see Introduction, pp. li–lix.

2 **onomatopoeia:** Onomatopoeia is often classified as one of a number of sub-categories of sound symbolism (also called 'imitative sound symbolism' – see Hinton et al. 1994, pp. 1–6).

3 **a word for 'little', or diminutive suffixes, are specially associated with vowel i, ï:** This 'fitness' of the /i/ sound for words associated with small size was noted by Jespersen (1922, p. 402) and played an important role in Sapir's experiments (1929). See also Introduction, p. liii.

4 **pratty:** A Middle English form of 'pretty' that has persisted in certain varieties of regional English, notably in midland, northern and Scottish dialects.

5 **micel:** Old English for 'big, large'

6 **katkaise:** According to Eliot's *A Finnish Grammar*, with which Tolkien was very familiar (see Introduction, p. xxiv), this is the '2nd sing.[ular] imperf.[ect]' of *katkaista*, to *break* or *sever*, stem *katkaise*' (1890, p. 265). Eliot's *Grammar* includes selected passages from Finnish literature. The note on *katkaise* refers to line

128 of Runo XL of the *Kalevala* (an extract of which Eliot includes) which reads 'Katkaise kala kaheksi!' (ibid., p. 264), translated as 'Cut the fish in two' (ibid., p. 265). Here, Vainamoinen asks Lemminkainen to cut in two a gigantic pike which is the reason why their ship has run aground.

7   **torri barf:** Welsh for (verb) shave, literally to cut/trim a/the beard (barf).

8   **trancher:** French for (verb) slice/cut/sever

9   **τέμνω (τμη, τομ):** Greek for (verb) cut/hew

10 **seco:** Latin for (verb) cut

11 **naddu:** Welsh for (verb) chisel/pare/whittle/hew/chase

12 **this "symbolism" played a part . . . and the notion or value dominates:** This idea is also briefly explored in 'A Secret Vice' (p. 15).

13 **fors:** Old Norse for 'waterfall'

14 **hávaði:** Old Norse for 'noise, tumult, loud self-assertion'

15 **the 'known languages' usually come to expression:** Tolkien explored this idea further in 'A Secret Vice', when he reflects on his own early language invention which was influenced by Latin, French, and other languages he learned as a child. See p. 14.

16 **Germanic group wōp – hrōp – hwōp (hwōt):** *wōp* and *hrōp* are Old English nouns for 'weeping' and 'clamour, lamentation' respectively. The two words are often used together as in *Ðǽr biþ á wóp and hróp* (there shall be ever weeping and wailing) in the *Blickling Homilies*. *Hwōp* is a root found in Germanic words such as *hwōpan*, meaning 'to threaten' in Old English, and 'to boast' in Gothic. *Hwot* is also a root in Gothic words such as *hwōta*, 'threat', and *hwōtjan/gahwōtjan*, 'to threaten'. Tolkien's continuous interest in this group of words is attested in his edition and translation of the Old English Exodus, in which he provides a note for 'hweop: hwopan' which 'seems to imply sound as well as menace' (*Exodus*, p. 69).

17 **cf. Barfield:** Tolkien is probably referring to Owen Barfield's *Poetic Diction*, which was published in 1928 and influenced

Tolkien's thought significantly. Barfield argued that in ancient times words embodied a perception of the world that implied a unity of physical and spiritual dimensions, and that in time words were gradually divided and sub-divided into narrower and narrower meanings. Tolkien sees a parallel here between unity of physical and spiritual perceptions and unity of form and content (the latter clearly points to sound symbolism). Tolkien notes that poetic words 'still' retain the unity between form (sound) and content (meaning) indicating that in the past there were many more words with the same unity that was later lost. This is also supported by his point above about the role of sound symbolism in the beginning of language. In later writings, Barfield explicitly included sound symbolism in his idea of the ancient unity of the word (see Introduction, pp. lvii–lix).

18 **Paget:** Sir Richard Arthur Surtees Paget, 2nd Baronet (1869–1955), was a barrister, scientific investigator and amateur speech scientist. His interest in the origin of speech led to the publication of two books, both appearing in 1930: *Human Speech: Some Observations, Experiments, and Conclusions as to the Nature, Origin, Purpose and Possible Improvement of Human Speech*, and *Babel: or, The Past, Present, and Future of Human Speech*. In both books he argued that human language originated in the imitation of hand and other bodily gestures by the human mouth, which in turn determined the production of sound, hence producing the phenomenon of sound symbolism. See also Introduction, xxxi. Tolkien could be referring to either book here, but probably the former, as this is the fuller study with a lengthier exposition of Paget's argument accompanied by detailed tables of words and diagrams of speech articulation.

19 **they take the words of modern recorded uncivilized languages:** Paget's *Human Speech* includes a great number of examples of sound symbolism not only from English and other Indo-European languages, but also from Semitic, Japonic, Oceanic

(Polynesian), and North and South American indigenous languages.

20 **wyrt wala:** Old English for the 'root of a plant'

21 **the 'fitness' is mostly a product . . . forms of this diverse group):** Here Tolkien seems to be referring to 'conventional sound symbolism', also known as 'clustering', in which certain phonemes and clusters are associated with certain meanings in a large group of words (e.g. the initial 'gl' in words such as glitter, glisten, glow, etc.) – see also Introduction, p. lvi. This is often thought to occur mainly by convention: the connection between sound and meaning in a few such words becomes so strong that many other words that share a similar sound or a similar meaning cluster together.

22 **in which thunner is from oblique thúr- > thour:** The word 'thunder' comes from Old English *þúr þunor*, which is also the cognate of the Scandinavian god Thor (the god of thunder). *Thunner* is a Scottish and northern dialect variation on 'thunder', clearly closer to the Old English original.

23 **muckle - mickle:** both are regional and archaic words that mean 'great, much, large'; *mickle* is chiefly found in the north of England, and *muckle* in Scotland.

24 **muckle - mickle in the proverb:** The proverb *many a little (also pickle) makes a mickle* is often attested in the garbled form *many a mickle makes a muckle*. Tolkien refers to this second, distorted form, first recorded in a quotation from 1793, which seems to originate in the misunderstanding that *mickle* and *muckle*, instead of variants of the same word, have opposite meanings, the former representing 'a small amount' and the latter 'a large amount'. This misunderstanding appears to confirm the hypothesis (referred to by Tolkien above, p. 65) that an /i/ sound is usually associated with smallness.

25 **Possibly weak for wook, or woke:** Tolkien here refers to the Old English adjective *wāc* ('weak, soft, feeble') which became *woke* or *wook* in Southern and Midlands Middle English. *Woke* was

superseded by *weak* in the fifteenth century (as it remains in modern English) and died out. Tolkien seems to have chosen this example because the form of the adjective that survived into Modern English has an /i/ sound, which is more apposite for its meaning – see note above.

26 **shift of meaning** with **phonetic shift** and presumably caused by it. (**mickle**): See note 24 above.

27 **das jüngste Gericht:** German for 'doomsday, Judgment Day, last judgment'

28 ***duni:** Old Germanic for 'loud noise'

29 **rook is no longer krāg or krāk or χrāk from which it took its use:** Tolkien is suggesting here that words used to signify the Old World gregarious crow (Corvus frugilegus) had always been onomatopoetic in origin, based on the sound this bird makes, usually rendered as 'kaah' (similar to the carrion crow but usually rather flatter in tone). Tolkien may have been inspired to restore some of the original onomatopoeic words that led to modern English 'rook'. In *The Hobbit* Tolkien gives two ravens the names Roäc and Carc (*Hobbit*, p. 235). Anderson notes that 'both these names are marvellously onomatopoeic invented names for birds in bird-speech' (2003, p. 316). Rateliff suggests that these names mirror the croaks the birds make 'roughly *rroahkk* and *kahrrkk*, respectively' (Rateliff 2007, p. 622).

30 **Lallwörter:** Also known as Lallnamen, lall words, lall names. Redin defines them as follows:

> By lall-words are meant such words as are formed by children in their earliest age, which accounts for the simple structure of these words. *A* is the most frequent vowel, the labials the most frequent consonants. Reduplication is common. Lall-words are an international linguistic phenomenon, and occur in almost identical forms in the most different quarters with the same sense, although there are exceptions to this rule. They naturally refer to persons and things that are of special importance to

infants, and accordingly the most common lall-words are those denoting parents or other relatives, e.g. Gr. μάμμη, μάμμα 'mamma', Lat. *mamma*, OSlav. *mama*, Lith. *māma*, Ir. *mam*; OHG *muoma* 'Muhme', Skr. *māma-h* 'uncle', Arm. *mam* 'grandmother'; Gr. πάππα 'papa', Lat. *pappa*; Skr. *tata* 'father', Gr. ἄττα, Lat. *atta*, Goth. *atta*. (1919, p. xxxi)

Early philologists, such as Max Müller, used evidence from such words to claim that all languages came from one, original proto-language. However, Johann Buschmann (1852) argued that they are rather independent inventions of children which are adopted into adult vocabulary, rather than handed down from generation to generation.

31 red karne – but elements in this are obvious: *Karne* means 'red' and is first found in *The Qenya Lexicon* under the root KṚN (*PE* 12, p. 48). This root later became KARAN and by the time Tolkien wrote 'The Etymologies' it was conceived as the origin of a series of related words for red, including Qenya 'karne' and Noldorin 'caran' (*Lost Road*, p. 362). Tolkien may be making a point here between the similarity of his invented Elvish word for red and the sound of words like 'carnation' which, while it evokes a type of red colour, actually derives from the Late Latin form *carnationem* (nominative *carnatio*) 'fleshiness', from Latin *caro* 'flesh'.

32 Phonetic predilection is rather that . . . the observed (or instant appreciated) facts: Here Tolkien defines 'phonetic predilection' which he seems to use as an equivalent term to the 'phonology' (the sound system) of a particular language.

33 štærks/scratch: Tolkien here gives the English word 'scratch', preceded by its reverse (phonetically, not an anagram based on spelling). No more explanation is given here, but this example was also used in 'A Secret Vice' (see p. 19) where its significance is revealed.

34 the pathetic fallacy scoffed at (but not explained) by Sweet in

the preface to his dictionary: Tolkien is probably referring here to Henry Sweet's *Student's Dictionary of Anglo-Saxon* (1897), in the Preface of which Sweet advises against 'etymological translation' or the use of archaic or obsolete English to translate Old English words when there is an alternative in common use (so Old English *bearn* should be translated as 'child', not 'bairn') (p. ix). Sweet repeats this idea in *The Practical Study of Languages* (1899) where he calls it the 'Etymological Fallacy'. Tolkien, whilst writing on philological matters nearly ten years later, was certainly in agreement with Sweet as evidenced in his 1940 essay 'On Translating Beowulf', in which Tolkien also mentions the term 'etymological fallacy' (*Monsters*, pp. 55–6). However, in the 'Essay on Phonetic Symbolism', he seems to be appreciating the contribution of the 'etymological fallacy' towards the attraction of the 'homogenous individuality' of a language. Interestingly, Tolkien here uses the term 'pathetic fallacy' rather than 'etymological fallacy'. 'Pathetic fallacy' is a term coined by nineteenth-century art critic John Ruskin and refers to an intense demonstration of emotion through personification of nature. Tolkien here is either misremembering Sweet's term, and therefore his use of 'pathetic fallacy' is just a slip; or perhaps he is using 'pathetic fallacy' in the more general sense of obscuring the object of contemplation through emotion, which seems to acknowledge the attraction to a particular language due to its homogeneity as an emotional response.

35 **to 'pure Saxon English':** It is possible that this is a reference to Elias Molee's *Pure Saxon English* (1890), one of a series of invented languages that were variations on a theme: the aspiration to create an IAL that speakers of Germanic languages would be able to learn easily and which would point to their shared Germanic background and tradition. This latter point was especially important – Molee used English as the basis of his IALs but 'cleansed' it of its Latinate vocabulary in an effort to return to the Anglo-Saxon roots of English, before it was diluted by

French following the Norman Conquest (Molee 1902, p. 9). Molee was clearly following in a long tradition of 'linguistic purism' in English. Attempts to purge the English vocabulary of Latinate and Greek-origin words by reviving obsolete words closer to Anglo-Saxon, or inventing new ones from Anglo-Saxon roots, go back to at least the later Middle Ages and became very significant in the sixteenth and seventeenth centuries. In the nineteenth century, William Barnes tried to 'anglo-saxonize' complex borrowed words of Victorian English (proposing 'speechcraft' for grammar, and 'birdlore' for ornithology), while Gerard Manley Hopkins and William Morris attempted to follow the same principle in their own literary compositions, choosing words of Anglo-Saxon or Germanic origin over classical-derived ones (Geers 2005, pp. 103–4). Tolkien was also partial to Anglo-Saxon-derived vocabulary, at least as a younger man. In the *King Edward's School Chronicle*, the report of a 1910 Debating Society meeting records that:

> J. R. R. Tolkien rose, and in a speech attempting to return to something of Saxon purity of diction, ("right English goodliness of speechcraft"?) deplored before the "worshipful fellows of the speechguild," the influx of polysyllabic barbarities which ousted the more honest if humbler native words. (Anon. 1910, p. 95)

Tolkien here adopts William Barnes' 'speechcraft' for 'grammar', invents 'speechguild' for the 'Debating Society' and defends 'native' diction. However, in his more mature academic work he cautioned against translating Old English using archaic or obsolete words of Germanic origin (see note 34 above).

36 the individual 'phonetic predilection' is not necessarily (perhaps never quite) identical with that of this system: Tolkien explores this idea further in 'A Secret Vice'; see pp. 24–5.

37 The divergence of the individual . . . one of the generators of "sound-change": This is quite an extraordinary view that Tolkien offers here, placing the *individual* phonetic instinct at the centre

of sound change in language. He touches upon a similar idea in 'A Secret Vice' and explores it further in his legendarium (see p. 26).

38 **where they are isolated they perish:** In the middle of the page, after the essay has ended, Tolkien has jotted down (in black ink this time) the words 'dum. dint. dent'.

PART III

The Manuscripts

[BODLEIAN TOLKIEN MS. 24 FOLIO 8:]

Folios 8 recto and 8 verso are part of the mini-booklet in which the 'Essay on Phonetic Symbolism' is written (see p. 3). They contain hasty notes for preceding parts of the essay written in pencil, which is very faint in places. Tolkien followed some of these notes very closely in the essay.

But only as a way

But I think it cannot be denied. This faculty exists and existed stronger once – Barfield.

It is still operative as a disturbing factor in both the course of <u>semantic</u> and <u>phonetic</u> inheritance.

here are perhaps notes from Paget. The word may be a loan or inheritance its adoption or persistence due to a feeling of fitness.

<u>reformation of inheritance</u> – if the only tradition{?} in choosing variants. <u>mickle</u> - <u>muckle</u>

Shift of meaning with phonetic shift. (again often only taking form if choosing from variants. as <u>doom</u> - gloom, loom, boom but bloom plume influence of l) This is sometimes not present <u>din</u> (but this is different in one usage{?} to <u>duni</u> although inherited contexts are still too strong for its natural association with tinckle, tin, ring. d is heavy).

Preservation of onomatopoeia. Probably false does not occur when the word has become a real word (<u>bleat</u>!) rook < <u>hrāg</u>

Preservation is due really{?} to reformation, or belongs to the quite special group of lall-worter¹ atta², baba, mama.

<u>Abstracts</u>, joy. Most inheriting is where we are most remote from onomatopoeia. Are such cases already connected mentally with <u>sound</u>. (merry gay)   <u>light</u>. The pleasure of L (some languages haven't got it) But same pleasure, light, jolly, delight, love, lovely, lesson, lists, belong, evil.

Sound preferences or play run on 'words' and independent of 'significance' – (<u>yes</u>.)

The individual 'phonetic constitution' or preference.

What makes Greek Greek?

No grammar of Gothic is complete without an attempt to analyse or at least point to some salient features which show (a) what makes <u>Gothic Gothic</u> as compared with the nearest relatives (Old High German) (b) what is 'Germanic' in it. This is particularly important in a language having a very clear and artistic phonetic individuality.   It is one of the reasons why people like old Germanic languages. {illeg} as recognized it lies behind the pathetic fallacy of 'pure English'   see Sweet

It is in the palate in every line of Homer. It gives Esperanto a value far exceeding other technically clearer and simpler inventions.

e.g. rare, substituting r for l containing the whole English system which is here {illeg} is met in English child.

The individual <u>not</u> as {illeg} as the community as lies a disturbing element. Sound laws are probably in one respect {illeg} of individual language which differ from those of a preceding generation. Those that are not shared perish. (But so strong is inheritance that to come to expression even conjoined or shared 'divergences' usually have to have secure foothold in the inheritance. ā > p But some violent changes do take place. {illeg} discussed l r + Hop. Others have built his work up (l d is Spanish) Old English ræs > æs

[BODLEIAN TOLKIEN MS. 24 FOLIO 25:]

Folios 25 recto and 25 verso: Notes on Jonathan Swift's *Gulliver's Travels*. Written in pencil on one leaf of 'Oxford paper' folded in two.

Gulliver 1726

<u>Swift</u>

Lilliputian[3]. tolgo phonac (fire arrows)[4] Hurgo a great lord; hek-
inah degul (cry of joy), borach mivola (look out down there)[5]
peplom selan (loosening cords)[6], Quinbus Flestrin the said
Flestrin Man Mountain, drurr 1/14 inch nardac[7];

Names   Lilliput, Belfaborac (French)[8] Mildendo[9] Clefrin
        Frelock, Marsi[10] –, Reldresal[11] Flimnap (Treasurer);
        Golbasto, Momaren, Evlame, Gurdilo, Shefin, Mully,
        Ully Gue (Emperor – satiric); Blefuscu[12] Skyresh,
        Bolgolam (Admiral)[13] Tramecksan & Slamecksan
        High and Low Heels[14] Limtoc (general) Lalcon
        (Chamberlain) Balmuff (grand justiciary {sic})

Blefuscu sprugs gold coin

Brob   gl gr lg[15]

Grildrig very little man[16] splacnuck (small animal)[17] glumgluffs
(54 miles)

Brobdingnag

Glumdalclitch[18] Lorbrulgrud (Pride of the Universe)[19]

Laputa[20]

clear smooth dialect not unlike in sound to Italian[21]

[BODLEIAN TOLKIEN MS. 24 FOLIO 37:]

Folios 37 recto and 37 verso: Miscellaneous notes. Written in pencil on a page of 'Oxford paper' torn in two.

<u>syntax</u>

<u>word form</u> and machinery attractive without necessarily profound novelty in syntax

hand-pleasure – writing for pleasure of hand & eye: this not really more rational than word making.

When it is <u>not</u> so engaging[22]

<u>menel</u>[23]

<u>kemen</u>[24]

Pagetism[25]

<u>not only fitness</u> but mere newness of relation. This pleasure exists{?} for change of vowel or sense.

<u>Novial</u>[26] dreary mass-produced. But it may come.

<u>ah seh vowel</u>

<u>fitness</u>

Personal make-up   It would require a good deal of research
to disentangle in any given person
(a) the congenital or personal
(b) the national or local sound
(c) the accidental: the product of learning of languages[27]

But it must be sometimes that (a) is operative through{?} (b)
and (c) as above.

Some people "take" to remote languages

I think every one as it were has their 'own potential' language.
But 1 language as we know it is not bespoke but ready-made.
We all wear ready-made dress we misfit to some degree.[28]

This one of the generators of change

Similar misfit in people of similar place blood & tongue habit.
Here greater importance of single language.[29]

[BODLEIAN TOLKIEN MS. 24 FOLIO 43:]

Folios 43 recto and 43 verso: Qenya poem 'Oilima Markirya', a ver-
sion of which is included in 'A Secret Vice'. Written in black ink on
a loose page of 'Oxford paper'.

Oilima Markirya

'The Last Ark'   first version

Kildo kirya ninqe ~~A white sh~~
pinilya wilwarindon
veasse lúnelinqe
talainen tinwelindon.

Vean falastanére
lótefalmarínen,
kirya kalliére
kulukalmalínen.

Súru laustanéro
taurelasselindon;
ondolin[30] ninqanéron
Silmeráno tindon.

Kaivo i sapsanta
Rána númetar,
mandulómi anta
móri Ambalar;
telumen tollanta
naiko lunganar.

Kaire laiqa'ondoisen
kirya; karnevaite
úri kilde hísen
níe nienaite,
ailissen oilimaisen
ala fuin oilimaite,
alkarissen oilimain;
ala fuin oilimaite
ailinisse alkarain.

The Last Ark

A white ship one saw, small like a butterfly,
upon the blue streams of the sea with
wings like stars.

The sea was loud with surf, with waves
crowned with flowers. The ship shone with
golden lights.

The wind rushed with noise like leaves of forests.
The rocks lay white shining in the silver moon.

As a corpse into the grave the moon went down
in the west; the East raised black shadows out of
Hell. The vault of heaven sagged upon the
tops of the hills.

The white ship lay upon the rocks; amid red
skies the Sun with wet eyes dropped tears of
mist, upon the last beaches after the last night
in the last rays of light – after the last night
upon the shining shore.

[BODLEIAN TOLKIEN MS. 24 FOLIO
44 RECTO and 45 RECTO:]

Folios 44 and 45: Miscellaneous notes. Written in black ink on a page of 'Oxford paper' torn in two. On the verso of both there are two tables of consonants for six different Elvish languages (see pp. 93–4 below).

own corpus

Fonway
aiþei[31]

Anna Livia Plurabelle[32].
Stream of consciousness[33].

A mere pattern visualized (without interpretation) – even from a point of view of normalities of visible word disjointed or artificial or 'monstrous'. Not possible with 'meaning'.
'Random thought' – is satanic and anarchic.

The three elements[34] should cohere and be in a coherent relationship one to another: but this does not of course suggest any one of them (least of all the 'meaning') is necessarily the most important in a given performance.

Merry Messenger

Normally 'meaning' – and/or at visual pictures are so strong that it needs as much training to listen independently or appreciated the independent contribution of the sound part, as to listen to certain subordinated parts of orchestrated music.

~~You can only listen to the~~ sound ~~with undisturbed clarity~~

Merry messenger[35]

Here the 'meaning' while coherent & having a little slender life of its own (which we may call if you like "atmosphere") – and coherently related to form – is so clearly subordinate to sound, that one necessarily pays chief attention to the latter[36].

But unfair to call it a mere 'metrical' experiment. One might call music a mere 'accompaniment'.

But with a traditional language 'pure sound' is impossible. All the "sound-groups" have senses (more or less definite) attached to them – their juxtaposition necessarily awakens the 'meaning'-~~sound~~ seeking faculty. And a pattern of those clashing woven meanings is necessarily made – even if it be bizarre or dream like.

We can pass to 'pure sound' only by writing 'articulate sounds' in measure – but sounds which have no 'meaning'. The music is their 'voice' – like a little tune on a ~~flute~~ whistle without accompaniment of voice or other instrument, some would say (though actually it is a great deal more subtle and intricate, even if attenuated than that). It needs an ear and training to appreciate it.

And even here the best results are achieved, because so tastes coherence and character in the sounds and their combinations achieved, by making a 'language' in which the sounds do 'mean' something (though only perhaps to the author)

[BODLEIAN TOLKIEN MS. 24 FOLIO 44 VERSO:][37]

Q.	p, t, k	Tel.	p, t, c.	N.	h, t, c.
	v, l, -		b, d, g.		b, d, g.
	f, s, h.		f, s, h.		f, th, h.
	m, n,		ɯ, n, g.		m, n, g
	s.		s.		h (s).
	w, l, r, y, -w.		v, l, r, j- v		gw, l, r, i - gw.

Dor.	f, t, c.	M.a.Ilk.	f, þ, h.	East.	p, t, ǧ (ku)
	b, d, g.		p, t, k.		b, d, ž (gu)
	b, d, g.		b, d, g.		b, d, ž (gu)
	m, n, g.		m, n, g.		m, n, ń (gu)
	s.		s		s
	gw, l, r, i̧ - gw.		w, l, r, j - w		v, l, r, v (- ɉe vo), v.

[BODLEIAN TOLKIEN MS. 24 FOLIO 45 VERSO:][38]

1	p.	t.	k.		p.	t.	k	1
2	b.	d.	g.		b.	d.	g	2
5	ƀ.	đ.	ȝ.		m	n	ŋ	3
4		s.				s,		4 (& ĭ, z)
3.	m.	n.	ŋ		ƀ	đ,	ȝ.	5
6.	u̯.	l, r.	i̯'		u̯	l, r.	i̯'	5 6

<u>aiþei</u>

Q.	p.	t.	g̱k	T.	p.	t.	c.	N.	þh.	t.	c.
	v.	l.	-.		b.	d.	g.		b.	d.	g.
	f.	s.	h.		f.	s.	h.		f.	th.	h.
		s.				s.					h.
	m	n	-		m.	n.	g.		m.	n.	g.
	w	l, r.	y, -		v.	l, r.	j, -		gw.	l, r.	i̯, —

94

[BODLEIAN TOLKIEN MS. 24 FOLIO 46 RECTO:]

Folio 46: Narqelion[39]. Qenya poem written in one leaf of loose 'Oxford paper' in black ink, with emendations and alternative lines in pencil.

Narqelion
(Paptaqelesta Lasselanta)

N · alalmeo[40] lalantila ne súme lasser pínear
Ve sangar voro úmear oïhta rámavòite malinar.
   Ai lintuilinda Lasselanta!
   Piliningwe súyer nalla qantar
   Kuruvar ya Karnevalinar
   v'ematte sinqi Eldamar[41]!

San rotsi simpetalla pinqe,
Sulimarya silda,[42] hiswa timpe
San sirilla ter in · aldar;
Lilta lie noldorinwa,
Ómalingwe lír'amaldar,
Sinqitalla laiqaninwa.

N · alalmino hyá lanta lasse,
torwa pior má tarasse;
lukalla sangar úmear
Oïhta rámavoite karneambarar

   Ai łe lindórea Lasselanta
   Nierme mintya náre qanta

~~San rot~~[43]
~~San pinqerotsin simpetallen~~
~~hwímer~~
~~súrimanen hiswa timpe~~
~~ter in aldali sir~~
~~sí~~ huín
San rotsin pirper simpetallen
~~súrimainen hiswe timpe~~
hiswa timpe Súrimo
~~San~~ ter aldalin sar hwíne
pinqe, lilta lie noldorin
Ómalingwe lir'amalde
~~Sinqeta~~
laiquninqva sinqeta

~~N · alalmeo lalantar~~[44]
Lalantar sí n · alalmeo me súme lassin píneën
Ve sanga voro úmea ~~oihta rámavoite~~ maloiwion rámaision
Ai! Lasselanta lintuilinda ~~pilinínen~~[45] ~~súsin nar sí qant~~ qanten
súsin nar pilinka
kuruvainen karmalainen
ve ~~sinqi yáva~~ yáva sinqi Eldamar

[BODLEIAN TOLKIEN MS. 24 FOLIOS 48–9:]

Folios 48–9: Miscellaneous notes. Written in pencil and black ink on one leaf of loose 'Oxford paper'.

A.

(2) individuals are more ingenious than the 'folk' – they could invent a better 'language'. But the 'folk' wins on wider experience. (+) And an individual creation comes up against others' 'phonematism'

(3) A language could be far better constructed in all technical points (phonetic grammatical morphological idiom) than it is by one man. Only others wouldn't accept it. Also one man (even with modern books) could hardly finish it – others would have to & the destructive process begin {sic}. He cannot foresee and provide for all words and combinations of words. He can present only a small part of experience – just as each language in a sense only presents one aspect of the external words – and the world would be poorer by the loss of each. Paradox. An artificial language could be richer, more beautiful than a natural, but world poorer by its acceptance. Let's have lots of beautiful artificial languages – garden flowers go wild. No need to be complete (Old English verse Old Norse)

Language is not entirely practical – playful, personal (as far as possible); indulges in an excess; incorporates mood with fact (though often though it is forgotten often to communicate mood is as practical, often more so, than to communicate fact.

[full fruition in verse – one must <u>construct</u> also a <u>verse</u> and a mythology or one's 'masterpiece' is incomplete]

(4) 'Poetry' is only constructable in a medium (1) you know well, exceedingly well, (2) which you cannot alter at will – the residuum of alterations of individuals is small & must even so correspond with exterior tendencies or knowledge or will simply seem harsh and strange. (can't change <u>heaven</u> into <u>hooven</u>)
    eida selda[46]

(+) Each individual probably has a 'phonematic form' or character but independent ultimately of his 'native' language[47] – languages influenced by it, and by learnt languages. The same is seen in languages themselves. This is expressed chiefly by <u>predilections</u> for certain sounds or by <u>combinations</u>, and <u>qualification</u> rather than actual phonetic individuality. A great deal of it survives 'transfiguration'

What makes Greek sound Greek[48] (Epaminondas)[49]

in construction – one comes across <u>phenomenon</u> of "fixation" <u>ma</u>, <u>ca</u>, <u>vru</u>[50]

<u>Gothic</u> <u>Novial</u>. Philological background.

<u>Spelling</u>.

B (1) Whence and why does beauty come in selection.

Hence the divided art of phonematic pleasure + semantic with their endless interactions – poetry

Simplest form of game / decide on the sounds and combinations / invent words according to the rules.

Others could enjoy these inventions as it is possible to enjoy and appreciate a foreign language – in the <u>process of learning</u>.

Our predilections for other languages, Spanish, Finnish, Greek, Gothic – in other moods Latin (Old English only because I know it so well) Distaste for French.

~~(1)~~ One would discover people belonging to different phonematic classes ~~to~~ speaking same native dialect – one of the roots of change.

Self handling

Tell me a man's language (in any sense) and I will tell you much else

Speech sounds are productive of "pleasure" which juxtaposes a total effect of sequences – similar probably (if different) to musical pleasure – air, melody. Not pleasurable merely or at all because of <u>musical</u> tone; but because of individual beauty (l r) or merely of contrast – yet total of human phonemes limited.

an art of making pretty noises (non musical) hardly impossible. Yet if one says a <u>beautiful name</u> bereft of association (Lostwithiel[51]). But these noises used for symbolising ideas. The form is there to give significance. It is now swung{?} round that non-significant sounds move us vaguely with a "significance".[52]

Points I would make are these –

There is what may be called a 'linguistic faculty' behind language – as one behind drawing: – though language is more often used with 'practical purpose' (so also but less drawing in writing, in maps plans etc.) it could be use{d} purely for 'amusement'. Divided art B (1)

~~The 'amusement' however~~

If one invented languages (in sketches or fragments of them) for the exercise of the faculty – the part that makes one choose right words word orders rhythms – the results would have more than one interest.

Scientific – 'phonematic' predilections and associations. Which is the limit in so called 'sound-symbolism'

Each individual a 'phonematic form'   A (1)

an inventor would play with here   .   A (2)

Individuals cleverer than 'folk'   A (3)

Poetry A (4)

~~The~~   Gertrude Stein[53]

Art word should mean something intelligible, but should have a
p Sound form. Correspondence between the two. The meaning
not necessarily "profound" – but more deeply felt. The sound
does it. Like reading something when music is going on (one or
other are deeply coloured). Abracadabra.[54]

[BODLEIAN TOLKIEN MS. 24 FOLIOS 50–2 RECTO:]

Folios 50–2 recto: Versions of the Noldorin poem (beginning
with 'Dir avosaith') and of the two Qenya poems ('Nieninqe' and
'Oilima Markirya') included in 'A Secret Vice'. Written in black ink
on loose pages of 'Oxford paper'.

Dir avosaith a gwaew hinar[55]
éngluid ~~ery~~ eryd argenaid
Dir tûmledin hin Nebrachar
yrch methail maethon ~~magradaid~~ magradhaid
~~Ð~~ Damrod dir hanach dalath benn
ven Sirion gar meilien
Gail Lúthien heb Eglavar[56]
Dir avosaith han ~~argenaid~~ Nebrachar

~~Lang~~ Like a wind dark through gloomy places
the 'Stonefaces' (Orcs) searched the mountains
over Tumlad. from Nebrachar (a place of goblins)
Orcs snuffling scented footsteps. Damrod (the
hunter) through the vale down the mountain slopes
to ~~her~~ awaited Sirion ~~whent~~ smiling. Luthien he
saw as a Fay from Fayland shining over the places above
Nebrachar

Norolinde pirukendea[57]
elle tande Nielikkilis,
tanya wende nieninqea

older vilyar[58]   yar[59] i vilya ti[60] anta miqilis   vilyen (nom
                                                                          plur)[61]

older – i older elle r   'N·oromandin in eller tande,
older wilwarindear   ar wingildin wilwarindeën
older qant'i lie   losselie telerinwa,
- older i/e -ar   tálin paptalasselindeën

Lightly tripping whirling lightly thither came little
Niéle, that maiden like a snowdrop, to whom the air
gives kisses. The wood-spirits (too) came thither,
and the foam-fays like butterflies, the white people
of the shores of Elfland, (with) feet like the music of
falling leaves.

Prose

Oilima Markirya[62]

Man kiluva kirya ninqe
oilima ailinello lúte,
níve qímari ringa ambar
ve maiwin qaine?

Man tiruva kirya ninqe
valkane wilwarindon
~~vear~~ lúnelinqe vear
tinwelindon talalínen,
vea falastam̃ ne
falma pustane

rámali tíne
kalma histane?

Man tenuva súru laustane
taurelasselindon,
ondoli ~~ninqe~~ losse karkane
~~ránar~~ silda-ránar
minga-ránar
lanta-ránar
ve kaivo-kalma;
húro ulmula,
mandu túma?

Man kiluva lómi sangane,
telume lungane
tollalinta ruste,
vea qalume
mandu ~~yape~~ yáme/a
aira móre ala tinwi
lante no lanta-mindon?

Man tiruva rusta kirya
laiqa ondolissen
nu karne vaiya
úri nienaite híse
píke assari silde
~~oilima~~ óresse oilima

~~Man kiluva oilima~~
hui oilima man kiluva

hui oilimante?[63]

<u>Man Kiluva</u>[64]

Peltakse[65]

Man kiluva kirya
ninqe oilima ailinello
lúte, nive qímari
ringa ambar

Man kiluva kir

Man kiluva Kirya
ninqe oilima ailinello ·
lúte níve qímari ringa
ambar

Rustom Pasha[66]

A A A ARTUR[67]

DÁIL EIREANN[68]
ÉIREANN[69]

ARTU[70]

ﺡ

TA ANLÁ –
FATA

[BODLEIAN TOLKIEN MS. 24 FOLIO 52 VERSO:]

Folio 52: Draft of the epilogue of 'A Secret Vice'. Written in pencil on one loose page of 'Oxford paper'.

> Mer hefir Sigurðr
> selda eiða
> eiða selda
> alla logna[71]
>
> euphony coherence not pretty – prettiness
> poetry produces beautiful effects with harsher medium
> Enkä lähe Inkerelle Penkerelle pänkerelle .   Kal xi. 55
> Ihveniä ahvenia Tuimenia taimenia   xlviii.10.

As an epilogue one may say this is not intended as a plea that such inventions satisfy all the instincts that go to make up poetry but that it abstracts certain of the pleasures of poetic composition (as far as I understand it) and sharpen them by making them more conscious. It is an attenuated emotion, but might be very piercing – this construction of sounds to give pleasure. The human phonetic system is a small ranged instrument compared with music (as it now is); yet it is an instrument and a delicate one.

But, of course, in so far as you construct your language on chosen principles – in so far as you fix it, and courageously abide by your own rules despite all the temptation to alter them for the assistance of this or that technical or expressional object or any given occasion – so far you write poet or may write poetry of a sort. Of a sort I maintain no further ~~remove~~ or very little further removed from your appreciation of ancient poetry (especially by a fragment recorded in Old Norse or Old English) or of your writing of it in ~~a~~ such a foreign idiom.

The subtleties of connotation cannot be there – your words have not had a real experience of the world sufficient to acquire this. ~~In such~~ In such cases as I have quoted above (Old Norse Old English) they are however at least equally absent. And in Latin and Greek to a certain extent.   But the ~~vague~~ less subtle tricks played by verse (or language-play of my hand) are possible as soon as you have even a ~~vague sense~~ general sense.

> green sun
> dead life

or <u>repetition</u>

These are common

language has both strengthened {the} imagination and been ~~strengthened~~ freed by it. Marvel of invention of the free adjective.

NOTES

1 **lall-worter:** for Lallwörter see note 30 to 'Essay on Phonetic Symbolism'.

2 **atta:** *Atta* means 'father' in Gothic. Tolkien's continuing interest in this word is evident from a 1958 letter to Christopher Tolkien (*Letters*, pp 261–5).

3 **Lilliputian:** The language spoken on the island of Lilliput in *Gulliver's Travels*. Lilliput was inhabited by a race of tiny people.

4 **tolgo phonac (fire arrows):** A command in Lilliputian which results in 'an Hundred Arrows discharged' on Gulliver's left hand (Swift 2005, p. 18).

5 **borach mivola (look out down there):** Lilliputian cry, warning people to 'stand out of the Way' (Swift 2005, p. 19).

6 **peplom selan (loosening cords):** While Gulliver lies immobilized, tied up by the tiny Lilliputians, he hears: 'a general Shout, with frequent Repetitions of the Words *Peplom Selan*; and I felt great numbers of People on my Left Side relaxing the Cords to such a Degree, that I was able to turn upon my right' (Swift 2005, p. 20).

7 **nardac:** Tolkien does not give a translation for this word, which is 'the highest title of honour' among the Lilliputians (Swift 2005, p. 47).

8 **Belfaborac (French):** The place where the palace of Lilliput stands (Swift 2005, p. 38). Tolkien seems to be pointing out that this word sounds French.

9 **Mildendo:** 'the Metropolis' of Lilliput (Swift 2005, p. 40).

10 **Clefrin Frelock, Marsi:** The exact name of the Lilliputian who signs Gulliver's inventory when he is arrested is 'Clefren Frelok, Marsi Frelock' (Swift 2005, p. 30).

11 **Reldresal:** Name of Lilliputian Principal secretary for Private affairs (Swift 2005, pp. 33–4).

12 **Blefuscu:** An island, 'the other great empire of the universe' (Swift 2005, p. 43), enemy of Lilliput.

13 **Skyresh**, **Bolgolam (Admiral):** Spelt as *Skyris Bolgolam* in *Gulliver's Travels* (Swift 2005, p. 60); the name of the High Admiral of Lilliput.

14 **Tramecksan & Slamecksan High and Low Heels:** The name of two competing parties in Lilliput who distinguish themselves 'from the high and low Heels on their Shoes' (Swift 2005, p. 42).

15 **Brob gl gr lg:** Tolkien abbreviates Brobdingnag, the name of the land of giants in *Gulliver's Travels*, and shows an interest in the presence of the consonant combinations /gl/, /gr/ and /lg/ in their language.

16 **Grildrig very little man:** The name given to Gulliver on Brobdingnag (where he is small) which Swift states is equivalent to the English *Mannikin* (Swift 2005, p. 86).

17 **splacnuck (small animal):** The name of an invented animal that the (now small) Gulliver is compared to on Brobdingrag: 'a *Splacknuck*, (an Animal in that Country very finely shaped, about six Foot long)' (Swift 2005, p. 88).

18 **Glumdalclitch:** A Brobdingnagian name meaning 'little Nurse' (Swift 2005, p. 86).

19 **Lorbrulgrud (Pride of the Universe):** Name for the Metropolis of Brobdingnag (Swift 2005, p. 90).

20 **Laputa:** A flying island Gulliver travels to.

21 **clear smooth dialect not unlike in sound to Italian:** A description of the language of Laputa. Here Tolkien seems to be quoting directly from Swift, bar two words, so perhaps from memory rather than having the text in front of him: 'At length one of them called out in a clear, polite, smooth Dialect, not unlike in Sound to the *Italian*' (Swift 2005, p. 145).

22 **When it is not so engaging:** This note is linked with an arrow to the word 'syntax' above.

23 **menel:** The Elvish word for the heavens, the apparent dome of the sky. It was formed from the roots MEN (direction, region)

and EL which is used for words having to do with stars (*PE* 17, p. 24). In Tolkien's legendarium it is used to designate 'heaven' 'the heavens' and 'the firmament' and is also found as an element in place-names; such as the name of the sacred mountain in the centre of the island of Númenor, 'Meneltarma', 'the pillar of heaven' (*Sauron Defeated*, p. 373).

24 **kemen**: The Elvish word for earth, in the sense of the ground beneath the heavens. This word may go back as far as Tolkien's name invention for his October 1914 adaptation of one of the key story cycles in the Finnish national poem, *Kalevala*. In his 'Story of Kullervo' Tolkien invented a name for Russia, which is called 'the great land' in *Kalevala*. The word he invented was 'Kemenūme' (see Higgins 2015, p. 77). The word 'kemen' would appear in *The Qenya Lexicon* glossed as 'soil' (*PE* 12, p. 46). In *The Book of Lost Tales*, the Vala of the Earth, Yavanna, is also called Kemi. This form would persist in Tolkien's development of the Elvish languages (see *Lost Road*, p. 363).

25 **Pagetism**: on Tolkien's objections to the work of Paget, see 'Essay on Phonetic Symbolism', p. 68.

26 **Novial**: IAL invented by Otto Jespersen; see Introduction, p. xliv. Tolkien's view about Novial in this note chimes with his (covert) comment in his 1932 letter to *The British Esperantist*: see Introduction, xlix–li.

27 **It would require a good deal of research . . . the product of learning of languages**: Tolkien's notes here correspond to 'A Secret Vice', pp. 24–5.

28 **language as we know it is not bespoke but ready-made. We all wear ready-made dress we misfit to some degree**: Tolkien included a very similar point in his O'Donnell lecture on 'English and Welsh', while elaborating his notion of a 'personal linguistic potential': 'Linguistically we all wear ready-made clothes, and our native language comes seldom to expression, save perhaps by pulling at the ready-made till it sits a little easier' (*Monsters*, p. 190).

29 This one of the <u>generators of change</u> ... single language: compare these notes with the ending of Tolkien's 'Essay on Phonetic Symbolism', p. 71.

30 ondolin: the last three letters are circled in pencil.

31 aiþei: Gothic for 'mother'

32 Anna Livia Plurabelle: Anna Livia is a character in James Joyce's experimental Modernist novel *Finnegans Wake*, which was published in 1939. Joyce started writing it roughly a year after the publication of *Ulysses* (1923) and during its long gestation he called it *Work in Progress*. Already from 1924, fragments from *Work in Progress* appeared in different publications. The section known as *Anna Livia Plurabelle* had already been published four times by the time Tolkien delivered 'A Secret Vice': 1) in the periodical *Navire D'Argent* (October 1925); 2) in the avant-garde journal *transition* (November 1927); 3) as a separate booklet by Crosby Gaige in New York in 1928; and 4) also as a booklet by Faber and Faber in London in 1930. Tolkien must have found Joyce's work (or perhaps only the name of this character) particularly striking, as he wrote 'Anna Livia Plurabelle' in his 'Qenya Alphabet' (later known as 'tengwar' letters) in a document dated 1931, now edited and published as a facsimile (with accompanying transliteration and commentary) in *Parma Eldalamberon* 20, pp. 87–9. Intriguingly, he has crossed out the name and has continued using the same alphabet to write his own name and address, as well as three liturgical prayers. According to the minutes of the Johnson Society, Joyce was mentioned in relation to 'eccentricities' of language in the discussion that followed Tolkien's delivery of 'A Secret Vice' (see Introduction, p. xxxiii).

33 Stream of consciousness: a literary technique that attempts to represent the flow of impressions, thought and feelings that pass through the mind. James Joyce's *Ulysses* and *Finnegans Wake* both rely on extensive use of this technique, often taking it to breaking point.

34 **The three elements:** visual representation of word in writing, sound of word, and meaning of word. See below.

35 <u>Merry messenger</u>**:** This refers to Tolkien's poem 'Errantry', first published in *The Oxford Magazine* in 1933 and later in *The Adventures of Tom Bombadil* (1962). As Christopher Tolkien has explained, the poem has a 'long and complex' history, and eventually evolved into two separate poems: 'Errantry' and Bilbo's song at Rivendell, as it appears in *The Lord of the Rings* (for a full comparative study of all versions and their variations see *Treason*, pp. 84–109). Evidently, Tolkien read the poem to the Inklings in the early 1930s and many years later he described it as a 'piece of verbal acrobatics and metrical high-jinks' (cited in *Treason*, p. 85). The published version in the *Oxford Magazine* and *The Adventures of Tom Bombadil* begins with the verses:

> There was a merry passenger,
> a messenger, a mariner:

However, early drafts of the poem begin rather with:

> There was a merry messenger,
> a passenger, an errander;

or

> There was a merry messenger,
> a passenger a mariner

(*Treason*, pp. 23–5)

36 **Here the 'meaning' . . . is so clearly subordinate to <u>sound</u>, that one necessarily pays chief attention to the latter:** Tolkien commented on 'Errantry' in his letters, often paying particular attention to its sound effects. In a 1952 letter to Rayner Unwin he refers to the poem's 'trisyllabic assonances or near-assonances' (*Letters*, p. 162); while in a 1966 letter to Donald Swann he mentions its metrical scheme 'with its trisyllabic near-rhymes', pointing out that the poem should be recited 'with great variations of speed.

It needs a reciter or chanter capable of producing the words with great clarity, but in places with great rapidity' (*Treason*, p. 85).

37 [BODLEIAN TOLKIEN MS. 24 FOLIO 44 VERSO]: In his letter to a potential publisher of both his 'Silmarillion' mythology and *The Lord of the Rings*, Tolkien indicated that 'behind my stories is now a nexus of languages (mostly only structurally sketched)' (*Letters*, p. 143). This table which forms half a sheet of Oxford paper (see p. 3) is a comparative outline of consonants in some of the various Elvish dialects Tolkien was developing in the 1930s and would find their full expression in his 1937 work *The Etymologies* and the related 'Tree of Tongues' (*Lost Road*, pp. 168–9). The other half of this sheet fits the description of a document published in *Parma Eldalamberon* 20, which contains transcriptions of miscellaneous materials from phonetic English into Tolkien's invented writing system, the Tengwar. The transcriptions include the Joycean name 'Anna Livia Plurabelle', Tolkien's name and address (which dates the paper to between 1930 and 1947), and the prayer 'Hail Mary Full of Grace' (*PE* 20, pp. 87–9). On this half sheet (which he struck through) Tolkien outlines the types of consonant shifts found in historical grammars for the Elvish dialects: Qenya (Q.), Telerin (Tel.), Noldorin (N.), Doriathrin (Dor. – this is the dialect of Doriath, the kingdom of Thingol and Melian), Ilkorin (M.a.Ilk.) and an Eastern dialect of Elvish (East.), which could be a version of the Fëanorian or Eastern dialect of Exilic Noldorin (*PE* 18, p. 27). The abbreviation M.a. before Ilkorin is puzzling; it may be that M.e. was intended, perhaps for Middle-earth.

38 [BODLEIAN TOLKIEN MS. 24 FOLIO 45 VERSO]: At the bottom half of this chart, Tolkien outlines the consonant groups for three Elvish languages: Qenya, Telerin and Noldorin. On the top half, Tolkien appears to have started sketching out two versions of a table showing 'Places of Articulation' of consonants: 1. Voiceless stops, 2. Voiced stops, 3. Voiced nasals, 4. Voiceless fricatives, 5. Voiced fricatives, 6. Liquids.

39 **Narqelion:** This is a version of the first poem Tolkien wrote in Qenya. This poem grew out of his composition process of another poem, in English, *Kortirion among the Trees* in November 1915 (*Lost Tales I*, pp. 36–9). Douglas A. Anderson has indicated that, presumably while composing *Kortirion among the Trees*, Tolkien wrote four lines in the upper margin of the paper in Qenya. He returned to these four lines in March 1916 when he completed *Narqelion* in Qenya (Douglas A. Anderson, email communication). The name 'Narqelion' itself is glossed in *The Qenya Lexicon* as 'Autumn' and is formed from the root NRQR, 'to wither, fade, shrivel' (*PE* 12, p. 68). This poem is a lament for the fading and loss of autumn and the coming of winter. The phonetic make-up of the Qenya words in *Narqelion* clearly show that Tolkien was attempting to create a link between sound aesthetic and semantics (see Introduction, p. xxii for examples of how Tolkien achieved this in specific lines and words of this poem). The version of *Narqelion* presented here offers a rare insight into Tolkien's process of imaginary language invention as in this page he gives different variations on the first two stanzas of the poem. This poem has been the subject of analysis by Tolkien scholars since four lines (not completely accurately transcribed) were published by Humphrey Carpenter (*Biography*, p. 76) and then subsequently in such journals as *Mythlore*, *Vinyar Tengwar* and *Parma Eldalamberon*. The most recent and detailed analysis of the poem accompanies a facsimile reproduction in *Vinyar Tengwar* by Christopher Gilson (1999, pp. 6–32).

40 **alalmeo:** This word replaces the earlier 'alalmino'.

41 **Eldamar:** see 'A Secret Vice', note 85.

42 **silda:** this word is circled in pencil.

43 **San rot:** The following 14 lines are written in pencil on the right-hand margin of the page.

44 **N alalmeo lalantar:** This and the following 6 lines are written in pencil at the bottom of the page, below the main poem.

45 **pilinínen:** This word replaces the earlier 'pileninen'.

46 **eida selda:** line from *Brot af Sigurðarkviða*. Tolkien praised four lines from the *Brot*, including this one, as having 'supreme vigour and economical force' (*Sigurd*, p. 233). See note 68 below for a further quote and commentary.

47 **Each individual probably has a 'phonematic form' or character but independent ultimately of his 'native' language:** Tolkien explores this idea further in the 'Essay on Phonetic Symbolism' (see p. 71) and in 'A Secret Vice' (see pp. 24–5)

48 **What makes Greek sound Greek:** The idea of a particular language's 'phonetic predilections' is explored in the 'Essay on Phonetic Symbolism', p. 71.

49 **(Epaminondas):** Greek general and statesman from Thebes (fourth century BC). In recently recovered recordings for the BBC documentary 'Tolkien in Oxford' (first broadcast in 1968), Tolkien noted that he first came across the different 'taste' of the Greek language by names such as '"Epaminondas", "Leonidas" and "Aristoteles"' and tried to invent 'a language which would incorporate a feeling of that' (quoted in Lee 2018, p. 136).

50 **phenomenon of "fixation" ma, ca, vru:** Tolkien examines the phenomenon of a language inventor's 'fixation' with a particular association of sound and meaning in 'A Secret Vice', pp. 18–19.

51 **Lostwithiel:** a small town in Cornwall, on the estuary of the river Fowey.

52 **an art of making pretty noises ... "significance":** This paragraph is linked with an arrow to the last section above, and is written vertically from bottom to top at the left-hand margin of the page.

53 **Gertrude Stein:** Gertrude Stein was an American avant-garde poet and novelist, and patron of the arts in the Parisian scene of the 1920s and 1930s. According to the minutes of the Johnson Society, her work was mentioned in relation to 'eccentricities' of language in the discussion that followed Tolkien's delivery of 'A Secret Vice' (see Introduction, p. xxxiii). Tolkien may have also heard about Stein in 1926, as two members of the Inklings attended her lecture

in Oxford. The Johnson Society had also heard a paper on Stein on 17 June 1928 (see Introduction, pp. lxi–lxii).

54 **Abracadabra:** A word-form that was believed by the Romans, Gnostics and Medieval practitioners of the occult to have magic powers when it was inscribed as a triangle on an amulet. The word itself has several potential origins: the form may have been invented by a second century AD Roman sage, Serenus Sammonicus, from the Greek word 'abraxas' which in the Greek system of alphabetic numerology is significant because it contains letters that add up to 365, the number of the days in the year. It may also have been Semitic in origin either signifying the words 'ab' (father) 'ben' (son), and 'ruach hakodesh' (holy spirit) or from the Aramaic 'avra kadavra' meaning 'it will be created in my words' or 'it comes to pass as it was spoken'. Over time that power of the word diminished and it became known as the incantation used in stage magic due to its sound aesthetic of being foreign and mystical (see Guile 2006, p. 2).

55 **Dir avosaith a gwaew hinar:** This is a version of the poem beginning with the same line that Tolkien included in 'A Secret Vice'; see p. 32.

56 **Gail Lúthien heb Eglavar/Luthien he saw as a Fay from Fayland:** In this version of the poem Tolkien translates the Noldorin word *gail* not as 'star' (as in the version included in 'A Secret Vice') but as 'fay' and *Eglavar* now changes from 'Elfland' to 'Fayland'. The Noldorin word *gail* is attested in *The Noldorin Word-Lists* as 'star' (*PE* 13, p. 143) and came into Noldorin directly from Gnomish as it is found in *The Gnomish Lexicon* with the same gloss (*PE* 11, p. 37). Tolkien uses the word 'fay' in the early versions of his legendarium. In the original 'Tale of Tinúviel' in *The Book of Lost Tales*, Lúthien's mother is described as 'a fay, a daughter of the Gods' (*Lost Tales II*, p. 10). Tolkien also describes the fading Elves in the Great Lands as 'fays' (*Lost Tales I*, p. 239). It may be, therefore, that this version of the poem represents an earlier stage of the Gnomish or Noldorin language.

57 **older vilyar:** the notes on this left-hand column are written in very faint pencil against specific lines of the main poem (in ink), as represented here.

58 **Norolinde pirukendea:** This is a version of the poem entitled 'Nieninqe' that Tolkien included in 'A Secret Vice'; see p. 30. Variations between this version and the one in 'A Secret Vice' have been noted and commented upon in *PE* 16, p. 95.

59 **yar:** This word replaces the earlier 'yan'.

60 **ti:** there is a bracket around 'ti' in red ink.

61 **vilisen (nom plur):** this note is written in very faint pencil against a specific line of the main poem, as represented here.

62 **Oilima Markirya:** This is a version of the poem with the same title Tolkien included in 'A Secret Vice'; see pp. 27–9. Tolkien has written the word 'prose' above the title, and Gilson, Welden and Hostetter have hypothesized that this term 'is perhaps meant only to describe the style of the poem, for while parts of it are rhythmical, nevertheless it differs from [other versions] in having no rhyme-scheme or regular metre, using the looser rhythms of prose instead' (*PE* 16, p. 55). This description of style is also valid for the other two versions of the poem presented in this volume.

63 **hui oilimante?:** this is written in pencil directly underneath 'hui oilima' and is probably an alternative form of these two words. Tolkien has also added a 'transpose' line that indicates that he was also contemplating the version 'oilimante hui'.

64 <u>Man Kiluva</u>: the notes starting with this line are on the right-hand margin of the page. Some are related to the poem, others seem entirely random (see notes on several of them).

65 **Peltakse:** This word seems unrelated to the poem. It is most likely a form of the Qenya word *peltas* meaning 'pivot', the plural of which is 'peltaksi' as found in *The Etymologies* (*Lost Road*, p. 380).

66 **Rustom Pasha:** a form of the name Rüstem Pasha Opuković (1500–1561), Ottoman Croatian statesman who served as the grand vizier of the sultan Suleiman the Magnificent and married one of the Sultan's daughters.

67 **ARTUR:** This is a form of the name Arthur.

68 **DÁIL EIREANN:** Irish for 'The Irish Assembly'. Note that an accent is missing from 'E' in the word 'Eireann' (compare with rendition below).

69 **ÉIREANN:** Irish for Ireland.

70 **ARTU:** This is a form of the name Arthur.

71 **Mer hefir Sigurðr ... alla logna:** Four lines from the *Brot of Sigurðarkviða*, the fragment of a lay of Sigurd of which only 20 lines are preserved. Tolkien translates these lines as follows:

> 'Evil wrought Sigurd
> oaths he swore me,
> oaths he swore me,
> all belied them; . . .'

(*S&G*, p. 168)

According to Christopher Tolkien's commentary in *The Legend of Sigurd and Gudrún*, Tolkien believed that the *Brot* fragment indicated the sad loss of 'an old and very vigorous poem' and he cites the four lines that appear here as having 'supreme vigour and economical force' (*Sigurd*, p. 233). Tolkien may have been thinking of using these lines here as another example of the power of the poetic form.

Coda: The Reception and Legacy of Tolkien's Invented Languages

The Reception of Tolkien's Invented Languages

The interlaced nature of Tolkien's language invention and his myth-making first came to readers through his two master-works, *The Hobbit* and *The Lord of the Rings*, arguably two of the greatest works of modern fantasy literature. Evidence of this language invention was seen primarily in the names Tolkien created for peoples, places and objects in his story. To many original readers these names may have appeared to have been made up randomly, but some readers may have noticed a consistent sound aesthetic to some of Tolkien's names. In fact, as noted in the Introduction, these 'made-up names' were actually coherent and had a solid morphological base, going all the way back to Tolkien's earliest language-invention in the spring of 1915. By the time Tolkien started working on *The Hobbit* in the early 1930s, he had already invented a 'nexus of languages' (*Letters*, p. 143) which gave his nomenclature a 'coherence and consistency' that he found lacking in 'other name-inventors' (see ibid., p. 26). Prior to 1937 and the publication of *The Hobbit*, Tolkien kept this language invention fairly private. He tended to downplay his own 'secret vice' to friends and family with such dismissive and self-deprecating statements as '[my] non-sense fairy language' (ibid., p. 8), 'unpublished inventions, known only to my family' (ibid., p. 21) and, as he wrote in 'A Secret Vice', 'the shame-faced revelation of specimens of my own more considered effort, the best I have done in limited leisure' (see p. 26). As shown earlier, it was only in the relative security of a small undergraduate society that Tolkien felt he could reveal his 'secret vice', still discussed with a fair amount of embarrassment and self-disparagement.

While *The Hobbit* from its earliest phase had been, arguably, connected to his 'Silmarillion' mythology (see Rateliff 2007), when it came to naming, Tolkien started off his narrative using more generic place-names (e.g. The Hill, Bag-End, The Water, the Misty Mountains) along the same lines as the names for places in fairy-tales (such as 'Fairy-land'). However, as he developed the narrative, Tolkien started to draw on his Elvish language invention for nomenclature. One of the earliest place-names that exhibit this is the name of the mines where Thorin's grandfather, Thrór, is killed by the goblin Azog: Moria. Moria is a Noldorin name meaning 'black-chasm' which made its first appearance in Tolkien's mythology in *The Hobbit* (see Rateliff 2007, pp. 80–1). Tolkien's names for his main characters in *The Hobbit* also initially give the impression that they were drawn from the primary world, especially from the myths and legends of the North which Tolkien so admired. For example, most of the names of the Dwarves and Gandalf's name were taken from the *Dvergatal*, a list of Dwarves in Old Norse found in the *Völuspá*, one of the poems of the *Poetic Edda*. However, the early drafts of *The Hobbit* show that Tolkien originally planned to call the wizard by a name drawn from his own languages, rather than Northern myth. The wizard who visits Bilbo in the original draft of *The Hobbit* ('The Pryftan Fragment') was originally named Bladorthin, a name invented by Tolkien from his earlier Gnomish and Noldorin languages, possibly meaning 'grey wanderer' (see Rateliff 2007, pp. 48–53). However, in the final text, this wizard's name would become the Norse-inspired Gandalf ('Wand-Elf'). The idea of the 'grey wanderer' would resurface during the writing of *The Lord of the Rings* when Tolkien would give Gandalf the Elvish name *Mithrandir*, which in Noldorin/Sindarin means 'grey wanderer'. Another early name that appears to be invented, and at the same time shows Tolkien's ludic use of language invention, is Golfimbul, the name of the Goblin whose head is said to have been struck off with a wooden club by Bilbo's ancestor, Bullroarer Took, in The Battle of Green Fields. Apparently, Tolkien originally planned to use the name Fingolfin for this Goblin (Rateliff 2007, p. 43), a name he had invented in the late 1920s for the father of Turgon of Gondolin, which emerged out of his work on 'The Lay of the Children of Húrin' (see *Lays*, p. 96 and *PE* 15, p. 63). When it came to re-using this name for the Goblin in *The Hobbit*, Tolkien became attracted to the 'golf' part of the invented name to playfully suggest the fate of the Goblin. As Gandalf tells Bilbo, the Goblin's head 'sailed a hundred yards through the air and went down a rabbit-hole, and in this way the battle was won and the game of Golf invented at the same moment' (*Hobbit*, p. 18). Tolkien decided to change the name to the more apparently comic Golfimbul, both driving home the joke and distancing it from the name of the Elvish king Fingolfin, whose role would increase in the version of the 'Silmarillion' Tolkien would develop in the 1930s (*The Quenta*).

After the encounter with the Trolls, Tolkien introduces several other names that came directly from his language invention. First, there is the name of the half-elven master of Rivendell, Elrond, who first appeared at the end of the 'Sketch of the Mythology' (*Shaping*, p. 38). Another example comes when Elrond indicates that the swords found by Bilbo and the Dwarves were not made by Trolls: 'They are old swords, very old swords of the High Elves of the West, my kin. They were made in Gondolin for the Goblin-wars' (*Hobbit*, p. 49). The place-name 'Gondolin' was one of the earliest ones Tolkien constructed in *The Book of Lost Tales* for the besieged Elvish kingdom that would be destroyed by the forces of Melko in his first great tale, 'The Fall of Gondolin' (*Lost Tales II*, pp. 144–220).

However, while there is evidence of Tolkien's language invention serving his nomenclature in *The Hobbit*, it was not until the publication of *The Fellowship of the Ring* in 1954 that readers were given the first longer samples of Tolkien's Elvish languages, including fragments of Elvish in poems and spoken dialogue. The reader first encounters this when the Hobbits, on their way to Rivendell, meet the company of the High Elf Gildor Inglorion who gives them shelter from the road and the pursuing Black Riders. Frodo thanks Gildor for his help with these words: '"I thank you indeed, Gildor Inglorion," said Frodo bowing, "*Elen síla lúmenn' omentielvo*, a star shines on the hour of our meeting," he added in the High-elven speech' (*Fellowship*, pp. 80–1). This is the first example of an Elvish language, in this case the High-elven language of Quenya, appearing as dialogue in the text. Tolkien translates the Elvish so the reader, if they so wished, could potentially engage with the structure of Tolkien's language invention. As the Hobbits journeyed further, Tolkien continued to add samples of his language invention to the narrative in both Quenya and Sindarin. In *The Fellowship of the Ring* this culminates in Galadriel's lament in Lórien '*Ai! laurië lantar lassi súrinen*' ('Ah! like gold fall the leaves in the wind!'), a 17-line poem composed in the

High-elven tongue Quenya with an accompanying English translation, which invited readers, if interested, to explore how the Quenya language related to English (*Fellowship*, pp. 377–8). More focused information on these and other invented languages, and the peoples who spoke them, would come to readers as paratexts in the final volume, *The Return of the King*, which contains two key appendices on Tolkien's languages: Appendix E, 'Writing and Spelling' and Appendix F, 'The Languages and Peoples of the Third Age'. As Tolkien linguist Carl Hostetter points out, the information on Tolkien's language invention in *The Lord of the Rings* and the appendices is 'scattered about and must be gathered up and correlated to make full use of it' (2007a, p. 2). In another piece, he states that the Elvish that readers encounter is 'almost entirely in the form of laments, hymns, poetry, spells, oath-taking, and the cries made *de profundis* and mostly therefore of a poetic or otherwise markedly formal nature' (2006, p. 232).

Early readers interested in Tolkien's languages started doing just what Hostetter describes: gathering up the information on the languages that could be gleaned from what Tolkien included in *The Lord of the Rings*. Even before the publication of the final volume, they began to write to Tolkien to ask for more information about his invented languages. One of the first to do so was the novelist and poet Naomi Mitchison (1897–1999), who read page proofs of the first two volumes of *The Lord of the Rings* and wrote to Tolkien with a number of questions about names and elements of the Elvish languages (*Letters*, pp. 173–181). Tolkien wrote back to her with answers, and noting that the questions she sent him 'will, I hope, guide me in choosing the kind of information to be provided (as promised) in an appendix' (p. 174). In 1955, Richard Jeffery wrote to Tolkien to ask for more information about specific Elvish words and place-names (*Letters*, pp. 223–4) and Tolkien took the opportunity to elaborate on several elements of his language invention. Some of the earliest Tolkien language aficionados in Britain were represented by the English author and scholar, Dr Rhona Beare, who started a correspondence with Tolkien and asked him several linguistic questions for this group (*Letters*, pp. 277–87, 307–8, 324–5). In a draft letter to H. Cotton Minchin from April 1956, Tolkien indicates that he had planned at one time to publish a 'specialist volume' which would be primarily linguistic in nature focusing on the Elvish found in *The Lord of the Rings* (*Letters*, pp. 247–8).[*]

In the 1960s, interest in Tolkien's language invention grew with the increase in popularity of *The Lord of the Rings* in America; due, in large part, to the publication of the less expensive paperback editions of the books. With the rise of Tolkien fan clubs and societies also came groups of aficionados who shared an interest in exploring Tolkien's languages further. Hostetter has appositely characterized one particular category of such fans as the 'decoders' (2007a, p. 3); those readers who attempted to find a 'code' for Tolkien's nomenclature, mainly by linking his invented names to the primary world, e.g. the name Sauron deriving from Old English 'sar' sickness (2007a, p. 3). Tolkien would address these attempts himself in the draft of an unfinished letter to a Mr Rang by dismissing any primary world associations for his names as 'no more than private amusements, and as such I have no right or power to object to them, though they are, I think, valueless for the elucidation or interpretation of my fiction' (*Letters*, pp. 379–80). Clearly, in this and other letters, Tolkien did not deny that he used

---

[*] A large part of this work was eventually published in 2007 in *Parma Eldalamberon* 17 as 'Words, Phrases and Passages in *The Lord of the Rings*'.

elements of primary world languages in his own invention but he clarified that these were usually selected due to their phonetic 'sound-sequence' (p. 380) and that their 'meaning' only came when the sounds of the words (or phonemes) were placed in the 'linguistic situation in my story' (p. 383).

In the 1960s and 1970s, information on Tolkien's languages increased with occasional publications in which he gave further information on his language invention. In 1967, he worked with the composer Donald Swann on the song cycle *The Road Goes Ever On*. This cycle was based on several of the poems from *The Lord of the Rings* and included *Namárië*, Galadriel's farewell lament in Quenya, for which Tolkien composed the tune himself, basing it on Gregorian plain-chant. The song book, first published in 1967, included linguistic notes by Tolkien on the Quenya in *Namárië* and the Sindarin evocation to Varda, *A Elbereth Gilthoniel*. Tolkien's notes include a word-by-word translation of these two poems, which allowed readers to see direct correspondences between the Elvish words and their English meanings (*Road*, pp. 65–74). Also in 1966–7, Tolkien included in a letter to the president of the newly formed Tolkien Society of America, Richard Plotz, a chart of two Quenya noun declensions: *lassë* (leaf) and *cirya* (ship) (see *VT* 28, pp. 1–40). This chart was subsequently made available to readers by being reproduced in several specialist Tolkien language journals of the time. In 1975, Christopher Tolkien released his father's guide on how *The Lord of the Rings* nomenclature should be translated into other languages, based on notes Tolkien made after the first foreign language publications of *The Lord of the Rings* in Swedish and Dutch. This document included further information on invented names and their meaning. In 1977, Christopher published *The Silmarillion* and followed this with *Unfinished Tales* (1980) and *The Letters of J.R.R. Tolkien* (1981), the last making publicly available many of the letters, mentioned above, in which Tolkien had answered questions from readers about his Elvish languages. In 1983–4 he inaugurated the *History of Middle-earth* series by publishing *The Book of Lost Tales*, the earliest drafts of Tolkien's mythology, which included an entirely new stage of language invention reaching back to the earliest forms of Quenya (then called Qenya) and the other Elvish language that would become Sindarin, Goldogrin or Gnomish. Starting in 1992, a group of Tolkien linguists, the Elvish Linguistic Fellowship (ELF), were entrusted by Christopher to edit and publish his father's numerous manuscripts of detailed linguistic material on the invented languages for his legendarium that were beyond the scope of *The History of Middle-earth* series. These were, and continue to be, issued in chronological order in the journals *Parma Eldalamberon* and *Vinyar Tengwar*. All this additional linguistic information clearly indicated that the Elvish languages of *The Lord of the Rings*, and related material, were not fixed and that Tolkien's language invention had been fluctuating throughout his lifelong work on his legendarium, a constant process of modification and change.

As this original linguistic material by Tolkien continued to surface, two different approaches to Tolkien's languages were also emerging. Each approach furthered interest in, and investigation of, Tolkien's imaginary languages and, with the advent of the Internet in the 1990s, became the subject of countless online user groups, mailing lists and websites.

The first approach aimed at studying Tolkien's languages in a descriptive way, treating them as a linguist would treat historical languages. Fans who took this view were ready to acknowledge, and consider as worthy of study, all the information Tolkien had provided about his languages at different periods of their development, even if the entire linguistic picture was complex and inconsistent. The foundational work of this first approach was, and remains, Jim Allan's *An Introduction to Elvish and to Other Tongues and Proper Names and Writing Systems of the Third Age of the Western Lands of Middle-earth as Set Forth in the Published Writings of Professor John Ronald Reuel Tolkien*, published in 1978. This edited volume contained some of the most significant linguistic analysis on Tolkien's languages by scholars such as Christopher Gilson, Laurence J. Krieg, Paula Marmor and Bill Welden. These scholars developed their articles for this volume from articles they had published in some of the earliest Tolkien language journals, such as early issues of *Parma Eldalamberon* and *Tolkien Language Notes*. The one drawback of this volume is that its data stopped at *The Lord of the Rings*; it did not take into account the new linguistic information that readers were afforded with the publication of *The Silmarillion* in 1977. However, *An Introduction to Elvish* was, and remains, of great value to Tolkien linguists due to the philological and comparative approach the contributors took when analysing the available material on Tolkien's languages. In 1980, the scholarship in Allan's book prompted several UK-based Tolkien linguists to publish *Quettar* (Quenya for 'Words'), the bulletin of the Linguistic Fellowship of the Tolkien Society, whose members were referred to as 'Quendili' ('lovers of language' or 'lovers of Quenya'). This journal used the linguistic methodologies found in Allan's volume to establish a scholarly practice for further exploration of Tolkien's languages (Hostetter 2007a, p. 9). In 1981 in America, Nancy Martsch began publishing *Beyond Bree*, the monthly newsletter of Mensa's Tolkien Special Interest Group. Martsch had a special interest in Tolkien's languages and from 1988 to 1990 she offered a serialized *Basic Quenya* course based on the version of the language found in *The Lord of the Rings*. In 1982, Paul Nolan Hyde inaugurated the column 'Quenti Lambardillion' ('Tales of the Language Enthusiasts') in the journal of the Mythopoeic Society, *Mythlore*. This column ran until 1992 and reflected Hyde's work on the compilation of a large, detailed, early computer database and index of all attested Elvish words in the – then – known corpus, which itself had begun as part of his doctoral dissertation (this was one of the first scholarly treatments of Tolkien's languages in a postgraduate thesis). Hyde's work produced several comprehensive glossaries and indices of Tolkien's languages, including the seven-volume *Working Tolkien Glossary* and the *Working Reverse Dictionary* (both 1989). In May 2002, the group entrusted by Christopher Tolkien to edit and publish his father's linguistic papers, the Elvish Linguistic Fellowship (ELF), launched their own online mailing list called *Lambengolmor* (Quenya for 'Loremasters of Tongues') which led to a series of high-quality articles in the online journal *Tengwestië* ('Language') on such subjects as Goldogrin and the Noldorin of *The Etymologies*. In 2006, Tolkien linguist and ELF member Carl Hostetter responded to attempts to develop an Elvish language that could be used for communication in 'Elvish as She Is Spoke' in which he disagreed with the attempt to conflate and homogenize different conceptual periods of Tolkien's language invention to produce a 'living language' that could be spoken (2006).

This is the hallmark of the second approach to Tolkien's languages; the attempt to 'use' Tolkien's imaginary languages as living ones. This second approach motivated author and teacher Ruth S. Noel's *The Languages of Middle-earth*, first published in 1974, and reprinted by Houghton Mifflin in 1980. In this 'handbook' Noel attempted to standardize and combine different forms of Tolkien's languages to offer the reader a uniform and more complete grammar and vocabulary in order 'to write, or speak original and meaningful grammatically correct Eldarin sentences' (Noel 1980, p. 60). Noel's work was used by fans to write and speak in Elvish, a pastime with which many Tolkien-related online forums and websites were occupied by the 1990s. In 1992, one of the members of the online forum 'Tolk-Lang', Anthony Appleyard, attempted to systematize Quenya grammar based on the new information that had come to light from the publication of *The History of Middle-earth* volumes, specifically the information from *The Etymologies*. In 1997, Helge Fauskanger launched his Tolkien language website, *Ardalambion*, aiming to provide standardized descriptions of Tolkien's languages. His website included original translations of prose and poems, including several books of the Bible, into a hybrid form of Tolkien's languages called 'Neo-Quenya' and 'Neo-Sindarin'. New words were invented for these two languages by using the roots Tolkien had created, as well as the sound shift rules that had been extracted from analysing Tolkien's linguistic corpus. This desire to 'speak' or write Tolkien's languages grew further with the advent of the Peter Jackson cinematic adaptations of *The Lord of the Rings* from 2000. Peter Jackson and Philippa Boyens decided early on, in the pre-production stage of the films, that dialogue in Elvish would be spoken. To invent this dialogue David Salo was hired to be the main Tolkien linguist for the three films and most recently for the three *Hobbit* films. Salo did most of his work via fax and letter e-mail and sent audio and videotapes of himself reading the Elvish dialogue he had constructed as guides for the actors speaking the relevant lines (Thompson 2007, p. 95). During the actual filming, Salo was on call day and night to construct more Elvish dialogue as well as lines in Dwarvish (Khuzdul), the Black Speech and Old English for the scenes in Rohan (ibid.,

p. 95). Salo also contributed to the level of detail and historic depth that Jackson's films sought to convey by developing Elvish scripts and runes for items such as Bilbo's sword, Sting, and the books of lore fleetingly glimpsed in Saruman's chamber in Isengard (ibid., p. 96). In 2004, Salo published *A Gateway to Sindarin*, a highly detailed account of Tolkien's Sindarin language.

Given the context of the reception of Tolkien's languages, both approaches have their merits as they each, in their own way, dig into the vast soup of linguistic invention that Tolkien left for the reader to explore, study and build upon. The first approach has led to the inclusion of academic articles of a high standard on Tolkien's languages in scholarly publications (for examples Flieger and Hostetter 2000 and Drout 2006) and has also encouraged many fans to become more interested in philology and the Germanic languages and literature Tolkien had a passion for. The second approach was instrumental in the growth of the languages outside of the context of the books and into fan-base communities. It was also crucial for the success of Peter Jackson's *Lord of the Rings* and *Hobbit* films, by bringing to the screen a vision of Middle-earth that alludes to the complexity and 'illusion of historicity' that Tolkien had created so masterfully.

Imaginary Languages for Fiction: Tolkien's Legacy

The impact of Tolkien's language invention would inspire other authors to incorporate invented languages into the fabric of their secondary world building. What would start out as modest attempts by individual authors of fantasy and science fiction to achieve this would ultimately become the domain of professional linguists hired by producers of motion pictures, television shows and computer games to include invented languages in the transmedia storytelling of such franchises as *Star Trek*, *Star Wars* and most recently George R.R. Martin's *Game of Thrones* series. Tolkien's work had played a crucial role in elevating language invention to a key part of inventing imaginary worlds, and those that followed used, and built upon, the models that Tolkien's lifelong language invention established.

One work that shows the clear influence of Tolkien's linguistic process is fantasy and science fiction writer Ursula Le Guin's *Always Coming Home* (1985). In *Always Coming Home* Le Guin depicts a group of humans called the Kesh and offers an extensive glossary of the Kesh language with an attendant Kesh alphabet which, like Tolkien's invented writing systems, was designed to work phonetically. The Kesh language is clearly agglutinative, building words and grammatical forms from roots, prefixes and suffixes (Higley 2007, p. 94). Le Guin also developed a series of punctuation marks for the language which indicated the correct intonation for words or entire phrases, thus showing interest in how the language sounded when spoken (Conley and Cain 2006, p. 11). Therefore, like Tolkien, Le Guin was concerned not only with the make-up of words and grammar but also with the aesthetics of the language sounds when read aloud.

Tolkien's principle of matching the sounds of an invented language with the characteristics and culture of its people is evident in the popular art-lang *Klingon*, spoken by the fictional Klingons in the *Star Trek* universe, one of the largest and most popular science fiction franchises that has been created around a secondary world (see Wolf 2012, pp. 134–7). Given the militaristic nature of the Klingon empire, the sound-aesthetic make-up of the language was focused on giving Klingon a hard, sharp, clipped sound, including the use of several guttural sounds like /H/ (as in the German or Welsh word 'bach') (see Okrand 1985). The inventor of Klingon, linguist Marc Okrand, also gave Klingon the uncommon syntactical pattern, Object-Verb-Subject (OVS), used by a very small number of natural languages, to further enhance its sense of strangeness. In a later book, *Star Trek: Klingon for the Galactic Traveller* (1997) Okrand offered even more information on Klingon (including various dialects and new vocabulary) and this expansion of the language motivated further world-building: he widened the culture of the Klingons via chapters on their history, mythology, cultures and society. Klingon, therefore, exemplifies Tolkien's principle of the 'coeval and congenital' arts of language invention and myth-making, this time set in a secondary world across various media, including books, television, computer games and films.

Other invented languages in such trans-medial narratives include *Pakuni*, developed by Professor of Linguistics Victoria Fromkin for the American television series *Land of the Lost* (1974–6) in which a family of modern explorers become trapped in a prehistoric alternative universe, ostensibly revising the age-old traveller's tale trope; and *Na'vi*, invented for the film *Avatar* by linguist Paul Frommer, also featuring in the trans-medial computer game *Avatar: The Game* (2009) which expands the secondary world of Pandora which the initial movie established. Language invention has also been used in creating dialogue and secondary world building for computer games, from the earliest text-based world-building games to the Massive Multiplayer Online Games (MMOGs) of today, like *Skyrim* and *Dragon Age*.

The most recent example of language invention for a secondary world is *Dothraki*, which was created for HBO's *Game of*

Thrones, the television adaption of George R.R. Martin's historical fantasy series *A Song of Ice and Fire*. In the novels, Dothraki is spoken by a population of Hun-like, loosely confederated tribes of horse-riding warriors who make their home on the steppes of Essos in the invented world of Westeros. In 2008, the creators of the HBO series approached the Language Creation Society about creating the Dothraki language which Martin had only briefly outlined in the novels (see Peterson 2015, pp. 89–90). A contest of linguists from around the world was launched to invent this language and David J. Peterson's 300-page Dothraki proposal was selected and he became the 'inventor' of the dialogue for the pilot to the HBO series (Peterson 2014, pp. 37–8). For the last season of the HBO series, Peterson also developed another invented language, *High Valyrian*, which again is only mentioned in Martin's original novels. As opposed to Dothraki, High Valyrian is meant to be a language used for learning and education among the nobility of Westeros (see Peterson 2015, pp. 35, 44), as well as in song and literature, not unlike the role that Tolkien's Quenya would play in the Third Age of Middle-earth in *The Lord of the Rings*.

The British fantasy author Terry Pratchett once said that:

Tolkien appears in the fantasy universe in the same way that Mount Fuji appeared in old Japanese prints. Sometimes small, in the distance, and sometimes big and close-to, and sometimes not there at all, and that's because the artist is standing on Mount Fuji. (Pratchett 2010)

Tolkien's legacy and influence on the invention of subsequent imaginary languages is evident and substantial. Post-Tolkienian invented languages follow and build upon the four key elements that Tolkien thought were important characteristics of invented languages. The first two, the creation of word forms that sound aesthetically pleasing and which demonstrate a sense of fitness between word form and meaning, are evident in many of the languages briefly surveyed above: Le Guin's *Kesh*, Okrand's *Klingon* and Peterson's *Dothraki* all use particular sound aesthetics to create word forms that convey meaning and may indicate the nature of the peoples who speak them. Tolkien's emphasis on the construction of elaborate grammars is evident in such publications as Okrand's *Klingon Dictionary* (1985) and Peterson's *Living Language Dothraki* (2014), giving readers quite extensive, unusual, and exotic grammatical information on these languages. Finally, the interlacing of language invention with myth, story-telling and secondary world building is now a natural element of fantasy fiction. Just as any fantasy world nowadays must have a map, it also must have elements of invented languages. What Tolkien may not have imagined when he first delivered 'A Secret Vice' is the sheer number of invented languages created for fiction (of all types) and also for purely private pleasure. *The Language Creation Society* (http://conlang.org) lists hundreds of language inventors, and books such as Mark Rosenfelder's *Language Construction Kit* (2010) and David Peterson's *The Art of Language Invention* (2015) give aspiring language inventors handbooks with which to invent new languages. Language invention has come a long way from Tolkien's 'hobby for the home', leading to the creation of 'neglected works in old drawers' – something that may have astounded and might well have pleased him.

APPENDICES

CHRONOLOGY

Date	Publications	Works in Progress	Related Events
1925	*Sir Gawain & the Green Knight* (edited with E.V. Gordon) 'Some Contributions to Middle-English Lexicography' in *Review of English Studies* 'Light as leaf on Lindentree' in *The Gryphon* 'The Devil's Coach-Horses' in *Review of English Studies* 'Tinfang Warble' and 'The Grey Bridge of Tavrobel' Inter-University Magazine (1927?) Contributes translation to Rhys Robert's 'Gerald of Wales and the Survival of the Welsh' (in *Transactions of the Honourable Society of Cymmrodorion: Session 1923–1924*)	Starts work on *The Lay of Leithian* (Summer 1925) works on to September 1931	Tolkien is appointed Professor of Anglo-Saxon, Pembroke College, Oxford

Date	Publications	Works in Progress	Related Events
1926	'Philology: General Works' in *The Year's Work in English Studies 5*	*Sketch of the Mythology* (The Earliest Silmarillion) – works on through 1930 Completes Prose Translation of *Beowulf*	Tolkien moves to 22 Northmoor Road, Oxford Gertrude Stein lectures at Oxford Forms 'Coalbiters' Norse Reading Group Meets C.S. Lewis (11 May 1926)
1927	'Philology: General Works' *in The Year's Work in English Studies 6* 'The Nameless Land' in *Realities: An Anthology of Verse* 'Adventures in Unnatural History and The Medieval Metres, being the Freaks of Fisiologus' in *The Stapeldon Magazine*	Writes *Roverandom* (Christmas 1927)	
1928	'Foreword' to W.E. Haigh's *A New Glossary of the Dialect of the Huddersfield District*		Otto Jespersen publishes Novial Owen Barfield publishes *Poetic Diction*
1929	'*Ancrene Wisse* and *Hali Meiðhad*' in *Essay and Studies*		Tolkien's daughter Priscilla is born

Date	Publications	Works in Progress	Related Events
1930	'The Oxford English School' in *The Oxford Magazine* (29 May 1930)	Composes 'Oilima Markirya', 'Nieninge and 'Earendel' (see pp. 27–9, 30, 30–32) Completes 'The Lay of Aotrou and Itroun' Tolkien starts writing down a story he has been telling his children called *The Hobbit.* Starts composing *The Quenta/Qenta Noldorinwa* and The First 'Silmarillion' Map (works on to 1937).	Moves to 20 Northmoor Road 22nd Annual Esperanto Congress held in Oxford (2–9 August)
1931	'Progress in Bimble Town' in *The Oxford Magazine*	Starts composing the two Norse poems that will be published as *The Legend of Sigurd and Gudrún.* Composes pages of Qenya Declensions and Word Lists.	16 May – delivers a paper to the Philological Society, Oxford, on 'Chaucer as a Philologist: *The Reeve's Tale*' Paget publishes *Human Speech* and *Babel: The Past, Present and Future of Human Speech* September – Addison's Walk with Lewis and Dyson 29 Nov. – delivers 'A Secret Vice' to the Samuel Johnson Society, Pembroke College, Oxford

Date	Publications	Works in Progress	Related Events
1932	'Sigelwara Land' (Part I) in *Medium Aevum*		
	'The Name "Nodens"' in *Report on the Excavation of the Prehistoric, Roman, and Post-Roman Site in Lydney Park, Gloucestershire*		
	'A Philologist on Esperanto' in *The British Esperantist*		
1933	'Errantry' in *The Oxford Magazine*	Starts composing *The Fall of Arthur*	

ABBREVIATIONS

AW	*Ancrene Riwle: Ancrene Wisse* (1962)
BBC Interview	'Now Read On', BBC Radio Interview (1970)
Bombadil	*The Adventures of Tom Bombadil* (2014)
ESMEA	*'Ancrene Wisse* and *Hali Meiðhad'* in *Essays and Studies by Members of the English Association* (1929)
Exodus	*The Old English Exodus* (1981)
Fall of Arthur	*The Fall of Arthur* (2013)
Father Christmas	*Letters from Father Christmas* (2009)
Fellowship	*The Fellowship of the Ring* (1954)
Hobbit	*The Hobbit* (1937)
Jewels	*The War of the Jewels* (1994)
Kullervo	*The Story of Kullervo* (2015)
Lays	*The Lays of Beleriand* (1985)
Letters	*The Letters of J.R.R. Tolkien: A Selection* (1981)
Lost Road	*The Lost Road and Other Writings* (1987)
Lost Tales I	*The Book of Lost Tales, Part One* (1983)
Lost Tales II	*The Book of Lost Tales, Part Two* (1984)
Monsters	*The Monsters and the Critics and Other Essays* (1983)
Oxford Magazine	'The Oxford English School' in *The Oxford Magazine* (1930)

Peoples	*The Peoples of Middle-earth* (1996)
Perilous Realm	*Tales from the Perilous Realm* (1997)
Reeve's Tale	'Chaucer as a Philologist: *The Reeve's Tale*', in *Transactions of the Philological Society* (1934)
Return	*The Return of the King* (1955)
Road	*The Road Goes Ever On* (1968)
Sauron Defeated	*Sauron Defeated* (1992)
Shaping	*The Shaping of Middle-earth* (1986)
Sigurd	*The Legend of Sigurd and Gudrún* (2009)
TOFS	*Tolkien: On Fairy-stories: Expanded Edition* (2008)
Treason	*The Treason of Isengard* (1989)
Two Towers	*The Two Towers* (1954)
Unfinished Tales	*Unfinished Tales of Númenor and Middle-earth* (1980)

WORKS ABOUT TOLKIEN

Artist	Hammond, Wayne G. and Scull, Christina (1995) *J.R.R. Tolkien: Artist & Illustrator.* London: HarperCollins.
Biography	Carpenter, Humphrey (1977) *J.R.R. Tolkien: A Biography.* London: George Allen & Unwin.
Chronology	Scull, Christina & Hammond, Wayne G. (2006) *The J.R.R. Tolkien Companion & Guide: Volume 1: Chronology.* London: HarperCollins
Reader's Guide	Scull, Christina & Hammond, Wayne G. (2006) *The J.R.R. Tolkien Companion & Guide: Volume 2: Reader's Guide.* London: HarperCollins

JOURNALS

PE	*Parma Eldalamberon*
VT	*Vinyar Tengwar*
YWES	*The Year's Work in English Studies*

BIBLIOGRAPHY

J.R.R. Tolkien's Works Cited in Chronological Order

Tolkien, J.R.R. (1924) 'Philology: General Works', *The Year's Work in English Studies*, 4, pp. 20–37.

Tolkien, J.R.R. with E.V. Gordon (1925) (eds.) *Sir Gawain & the Green Knight*. Oxford: Clarendon Press.

Tolkien J.R.R. (1926) 'Philology: General Works', *The Year's Work in English Studies*, 5, pp. 26–65.

Tolkien, J.R.R. (1927) 'Philology: General Works', *The Year's Work in English Studies*, 6, pp. 32–66.

Tolkien, J.R.R. (1927) 'Adventures in Unnatural History and the Medieval Metres, being The Freaks of Fisiologus', *The Stapledon Magazine*, 7, p. 40.

Tolkien, J.R.R (1929) '*Ancrene Wisse* and *Hali Meiðhad*', *Essays and Studies by Members of the English Association*, 14, pp. 104–26.

Tolkien, J.R.R. (1930) 'The Oxford English School', *The Oxford Magazine*, 29 May 1930, pp. 778–82.

Tolkien, J.R.R. (1934) 'Chaucer as a Philologist: *The Reeve's Tale*', *Transactions of the Philological Society*, 33: 1, pp. 1–70.

Tolkien, J.R.R. (2007 [1937]) *The Hobbit*. London: George Allen & Unwin (cited here from 70th Anniversary Edition, London: HarperCollins, 2007).

The Lord of the Rings in three volumes:

Tolkien, J.R.R. (2004 [1954]) *The Fellowship of the Ring*. London: George Allen & Unwin (cited here from 50th Anniversary Edition, edited by Wayne G. Hammond & Christina Scull, London: HarperCollins, 2004).

Tolkien, J.R.R. (2004 [1954]) *The Two Towers*. London: George Allen & Unwin, 1954 (cited here from 50th Anniversary Edition, edited by Wayne G. Hammond & Christina Scull, London: HarperCollins, 2004).

Tolkien, J.R.R. (2004 [1955]) *The Return of the King*. London: George Allen & Unwin (cited here from 50th Anniversary Edition, edited by Wayne G. Hammond & Christina Scull, London: HarperCollins, 2004).

Tolkien, J.R.R. (1962) (ed.) *The English Text of the Ancrene Riwle: Ancrene Wisse, edited from MS. Corpus Christi College Cambridge 402*. London: Oxford University Press.

Tolkien, J.R.R. (1968 [1967]) *The Road Goes Ever On: A Song Cycle, Music by Donald Swann, Poems by J.R.R. Tolkien*. London: George Allen & Unwin.

Tolkien, J.R.R. (1970) *Now Read On*, BBC Radio Interview, Denys Gueroult and J.R.R. Tolkien, December 16, 1970, Marquette University Tolkien Archive, JRRT 5/2/9.

Tolkien, J.R.R. (1976, revised as *Letters from Father Christmas* 1999) *The Father Christmas Letters*, edited by Baillie Tolkien. London: HarperCollins.

Tolkien, J.R.R. (1977) *The Silmarillion*, edited by Christopher Tolkien. London: George Allen & Unwin.

Tolkien, J.R.R. (1980) *Unfinished Tales of Númenor and Middle-earth*, edited by Christopher Tolkien. London: George Allen & Unwin.

Tolkien, J.R.R. (1981) *The Letters of J.R.R. Tolkien*, edited by

Humphrey Carpenter, with the assistance of Christopher Tolkien. London: George Allen & Unwin.

Tolkien, J.R.R. (1981) *The Old English Exodus: Text, Translation and Commentary*, edited by Joan Turville-Petre. Oxford: Clarendon Press.

Tolkien, J.R.R. (1982) *The Monsters and the Critics and Other Essays*, edited by Christopher Tolkien. London: George Allen & Unwin.

Tolkien, J.R.R. (1983) *The Book of Lost Tales, Part One*, edited by Christopher Tolkien. London: George Allen & Unwin.

Tolkien, J.R.R. (1984) *The Book of Lost Tales, Part Two*, edited by Christopher Tolkien. London: George Allen & Unwin.

Tolkien, J.R.R. (1985) *The Lays of Beleriand*, edited by Christopher Tolkien. London: George Allen & Unwin.

Tolkien, J.R.R. (1986) *The Shaping of Middle-earth*, edited by Christopher Tolkien. London: George Allen & Unwin.

Tolkien, J.R.R. (1987) *The Lost Road and Other Writings*, edited by Christopher Tolkien. London: Unwin Hyman.

Tolkien, J.R.R. (1988) *The Return of the Shadow: The History of The Lord of the Rings, Part One*, edited by Christopher Tolkien. London: Unwin Hyman.

Tolkien, J.R.R. (1989) *The Treason of Isengard: The History of The Lord of the Rings, Part Two*, edited by Christopher Tolkien. London: Unwin Hyman.

Tolkien, J.R.R. (1990) *The War of the Ring: The History of The Lord of the Rings, Part Three*, edited by Christopher Tolkien. London: Unwin Hyman.

Tolkien, J.R.R. (1990) 'The Elves at Koivienéni: A New Qenya Sentence', edited by Christopher Gilson and Patrick H. Wynne, *Vinyar Tengwar*, 14, pp. 1–24.

Tolkien, J.R.R. (1992) *Sauron Defeated: The End of the The Third Age*, edited by Christopher Tokien. London: HarperCollins.

Tolkien, J.R.R. (1993) 'The Bodleian Declensions', edited by

Christopher Gilson, Patrick H. Wynne, and Carl F. Hostetter, *Vinyar Tengwar*, 28, pp. 1–40.

Tolkien, J.R.R. (1993) *Morgoth's Ring: The Later Silmarillion, Part One: The Legends of Aman*, edited by Christopher Tolkien. London: HarperCollins.

Tolkien, J.R.R. (1994) *The War of the Jewels: The Later Silmarillion, Part Two: The Legends of Beleriand*, edited by Christopher Tolkien. London: HarperCollins.

Tolkien, J.R.R. (1995) 'I·Lam na·Ngoldathon: The Grammar and Lexicon of the Gnomish Tongue', edited by Christopher Gilson, Patrick Wynne, Arden R. Smith and Carl F. Hostetter, *Parma Eldalamberon*, 11 (*PE* 11).

Tolkien, J.R.R. (1996) *The Peoples of Middle-earth*, edited by Christopher Tolkien. London: HarperCollins.

Tolkien, J.R.R. (1997) *Tales from the Perilous Realm*. London: HarperCollins.

Tolkien, J.R.R. (1998) 'Qenyaqetsa: The Qenya Phonology and Lexicon: together with The Poetic and Mythologic Words of Eldarissa', edited by Christopher Gilson, Carl F. Hostetter, Patrick Wynne and Arden R. Smith, *Parma Eldalamberon*, 12, pp. 1–112 (*PE* 12).

Tolkien, J.R.R. (2001) 'The Alphabet of Rúmil & Early Noldorin Fragments', edited by Arden R. Smith, Christopher Gilson, Bill Welden, Carl F. Hostetter and Patrick Wynne, *Parma Eldalamberon*, 13 (*PE* 13).

Tolkien, J.R.R. (2003) 'Early Qenya Fragments & Grammar and The Valmaric Script', edited by Patrick Wynne, Christopher Gilson, Carl F. Hostetter, Bill Welden and Arden R. Smith, *Parma Eldalamberon*, 14 (*PE* 14).

Tolkien, J.R.R. (2004) 'Sí Qente Feanor and Other Elvish Writings', edited by Arden R. Smith, Christopher Gilson, Patrick H. Wynne and Bill Welden, *Parma Eldalamberon*, 15 (PE 15).

Tolkien, J.R.R. (2006) 'Early Elvish Poetry and Pre-Fëanorian Alphabets', edited by Christopher Gilson, Arden R. Smith, Patrick H. Wynne, Carl F. Hostetter and Bill Welden, *Parma Eldalamberon*, 16 (PE 16).

Tolkien, J.R.R. (2007) 'Words Phrases and Passages in *The Lord of the Rings*', edited by Christopher Gilson, *Parma Eldalamberon*, 17 (PE 17).

Tolkien, J.R.R. (2008) *Tolkien On Fairy-stories*, edited by Verlyn Flieger and Douglas A. Anderson. London: HarperCollins.

Tolkien, J.R.R. (2009) *The Legend of Sigurd and Gudrún*, edited by Christopher Tolkien. London: HarperCollins.

Tolkien, J.R.R. (2009) 'Tengwesta Qenderinwa', edited by Christoper Gilson and Patrick H. Wynne, *Parma Eldalamberon*, 18 (PE 18).

Tolkien, J.R.R. (2012) 'The Qenya Alphabet', edited by Arden R. Smith, *Parma Eldalamberon*, 20 (PE 20).

Tolkien, J.R.R. (2013) *The Fall of Arthur*, edited by Christopher Tolkien. London: HarperCollins.

Tolkien, J.R.R. (2014) *The Adventures of Tom Bombadil*, edited by Christina Scull and Wayne G. Hammond. London: HarperCollins.

Tolkien, J.R.R. (2015) *The Story of Kullervo*, edited by Verlyn Flieger. London: HarperCollins.

MATERIALS FROM ARCHIVES

Pembroke College Archives Catalogue

Pembroke College Archives, Johnson Society Minute Book, PMB/R/6/1/6 1927–1929

Pembroke College Archives, Johnson Society Minute Book, PMB/R/6/1/7 1929–1937)

Exeter College Archives, Esperanto Club

DICTIONARIES CONSULTED

Balg, Gerhard Hubert (1887) (ed.) A comparative glossary of the Gothic language with especial reference to English and German. London: Truebner & Co.

Bosworth, Joseph and Toller, T. Northcote (1882–98) (eds.) *An Anglo-Saxon Dictionary based on the manuscript collections of the late Joseph Bosworth, edited and enlarged by T. Northcote Toller.* Oxford: Clarendon Press.

Cleasby, Richard and Vigfússon, Gudbrand (1874) (eds.) *An Icelandic-English dictionary, based on the ms. collections of the late Richard Cleasby. Enl. and completed by Gudbrand Vigfússon.* Oxford: Clarendon Press.

Oxford English Dictionary Online. Oxford University Press. Available at: http://www.oed.com/ (Accessed on 31 May 2015).

OTHER WORKS CITED

Allan, Jim (1978) *An Introduction To Elvish.* Hayes, Middlesex: Bran's Head Press.

Anderson, Douglas A. (2003) *The Annotated Hobbit,* Revised and Expanded Edition. London: HarperCollins.

Anderson, Douglas A. (2005) 'J.R.R. Tolkien and W. Rhys Roberts's "Gerald of Wales on the Survival of Welsh"', *Tolkien Studies,* 2, pp. 230–4.

Anderson, Earl R. (1998) *A Grammar of Iconism.* Madison, NJ; London: Fairleigh Dickinson University Press; Associated University Presses.

Anon. (1910) 'Debating Society', *King Edward's School Chronicle,* 25, pp. 94–5.

Anon. (1930) *XXIIa Universala Kongreso de Esperanto En Oxford Kongresa Libro.* Oxford.

Barfield, Owen (1973 [1928]) *Poetic Diction: A Study in Meaning.* Middletown, Wesleyan University Press.

Barfield, Owen (1988 [1957]) *Saving the Appearances: A Study in Idolatry.* Middletown, CT: Wesleyan University Press.

Bishop, John (1986) *Joyce's Book of the Dark: Finnegans Wake.* Madison, Wisconsin: University of Wisconsin Press.

Bloomfield, Leonard (1909) *A Semasiological Differentiation in Germanic Secondary Ablaut.* Chicago: The University of Chicago.

Bulwer-Lytton, Edward (2009 [1871]) *Vril: The Power of the Coming Race.* New York: CreateSpace.

Bratman, David (2001) 'R.B. McCallum: The Master Inkling', *Mythlore*, 23:3, pp. 34–42.

Buschmann, Johann C. E. (1852) 'Über den Naturlaut', *Philologische und Historische Abhandlungen der Königlichen Akademie der Wissenschaft zu Berlin*, 3, pp. 391–423.

Carpenter, Humphrey (1978) *The Inklings: C.S. Lewis, J.R.R. Tolkien, Charles Williams and Their Friends.* London: George Allen & Unwin.

Cilli, Oronzo (2014) *The Educational Value of Esperanto: The Word of Tolkien in The British Esperantist 1933.* Available at: http://tolkieniano.blogspot.co.uk/2014/03/the-educational-value-of-esperanto-word.html (Accessed on: 31 May 2015).

Conley, T. and Cain, S. (eds.) (2006) *Encyclopedia of Fictional and Fantastic Languages.* London: Greenwood Press.

Croft, Janet Brennan (2007) 'Walter E. Haigh, Author of *A New Glossary of the Huddersfield Dialect*', *Tolkien Studies*, 4, pp. 184–8.

Drout, Michael D.C. (ed.) (2007), *J.R.R. Tolkien Encyclopedia: Scholarship and Critical Assessment.* New York: Routledge.

Dydo, Ulla E. (2003) *Gertrude Stein: The Language That Rises: 1923–1934.* Evanston, Ill.: Northwestern University Press.

Eco, Umberto (1995) *The Search for the Perfect Language*, translated by James Fentress. Oxford: Blackwell.

Eliot, C.N.E. (1890) *A Finnish Grammar*. Oxford: Clarendon Press.

Ellmann, Richard (1983) *James Joyce*. Oxford: Oxford University Press.

Etzel, Stefan (1983) *Untersuchungen zur Lautsymbolik*. Unpublished PhD Thesis: University of Frankfurt am Main.

Falk, Julia S. (1992) 'Otto Jespersen, Leonard Bloomfield, and American Structural Linguistics', *Language*, 68:3, pp. 465–91.

Fimi, Dimitra (2008) *Tolkien, Race and Cultural History: From Fairies to Hobbits*. London: Palgrave Macmillan.

Flieger, Verlyn (1981) 'Barfield's Poetic Diction and Splintered Light', *Studies in the Literary Imagination*, 14:2, pp. 47–66.

Flieger, Verlyn (2002 [1983]) *Splintered Light: Logos and Language in Tolkien's World*, Kent, Ohio: Kent State University Press.

Flieger, Verlyn (2007) 'Barfield, Owen (1898–1997)', in Drout, Michael D.C. (ed.) *J.R.R. Tolkien Encyclopedia: Scholarship and Critical Assessment*. New York: Routledge, pp. 50–1.

Flieger, Verlyn and Hostetter, Carl F. (eds.) (2000) *Tolkien's Legendarium: Essays on The History of Middle-earth*. Westport, London: Greenwood Press.

Geers, Maria (2005) 'A Comparative Study of Linguistic Purism in the History of England and Germany', in Langer, Nils and Davies, Winifred V. (eds.) *Linguistic Purism in the Germanic Languages*. Berlin: Walter de Gruyter, pp. 97–108.

Genette, Gérard (1995) *Mimologics = Mimologiques: Voyage en Cratylie*, translated by Thaïs E. Morgan; with a foreword by Gerald Prince. Lincoln; London: University of Nebraska.

Gilson, Christopher (1999) 'Narqelion and the Early Lexicons: Some Notes on the First Elvish Poem', *Vinyar Tengwar*, 40, pp. 6–33.

Glyer, Diana Pavlac (2007) *The Company They Keep: C.S. Lewis and J. R. R. Tolkien as Writers in Community*. Kent, Ohio: Kent State University Press.

Greg, Percy (1880) *Across the Zodiac: The Story of A Wrecked Record*. London: Trubner Company.

Gregor, D.B. (1982) *La Fontoj de Esperanto*. Glasgow: Kardo.

Guile, Rosemary (2006) *The Encyclopedia of Magic and Alchemy*. New York: Facts on File.

Higgins, Andrew (2015) *The Genesis of Tolkien's Mythology*. Unpublished PhD Thesis: Cardiff Metropolitan University.

Higley, Sarah (2007) *Hildegard of Bingen's Unknown Language: An Edition, Translation, and Discussion*. London: Palgrave Macmillan.

Hinton, Leanne, Nichols, Johanna and Ohala, John J. (eds.) (1994) *Sound Symbolism*. Cambridge; New York: Cambridge University Press.

Hostetter, Carl F. (2006) '"Elvish as She Is Spoke"', in Hammond, Wayne G. and Scull, Christina (eds.) *The Lord of the Rings 1954–2004: Scholarship in Honor of Richard E. Blackwelder*. Milwaukee, Wisconsin: Marquette University Press, pp. 231–55.

Hostetter, Carl F. (2007a) 'Tolkienian Linguistics: The First Fifty Years', *Tolkien Studies*, 4, pp. 1–46.

Hostetter, Carl F. (2007b) 'Languages Invented by Tolkien', in Drout, Michael D.C. (ed.) *J.R.R. Tolkien Encyclopedia: Scholarship and Critical Assessment*. New York: Routledge, pp. 332–44.

Jespersen, Otto (1922) *Language: Its Nature, Development and Origin*. London: George Allen & Unwin.

Jespersen, Otto (1929) 'Nature and Art in Language', *American Speech*, 5, pp. 89–103.

Joyce, James (1922) *Ulysses*. Paris: Shakespeare & Co.; Sylvia Beach.

Joyce, James (1939) *Finnegans Wake*. London: Faber & Faber.

Kahlas-Tarkka, Leena (2014) 'Finnish: The Land and Language of Heroes', in Lee, Stuart D. (ed.) *A Companion to J.R.R. Tolkien*. Chichester: Wiley Blackwell, pp. 259–71.

Körtvélyessy, Lívia (2015) *Evaluative Morphology from a Cross-Linguistic Perspective*. Newcastle upon Tyne: Cambridge Scholars Publishing, 2015.

Lear, Edward (2002), *The Compete Nonsense and Other Verse*. New York: Penguin Classics.

Le Guin, Ursula K. (1985) *Always Coming Home*. New York: Harper and Row.

Lee, Stuart (2018) '"Tolkien in Oxford" (BBC, 1968):h A Reconstruction', *Tolkien Studies*, 15, pp. 115–76.

Leick, Karen (2009) *Gertrude Stein and the Making of an American Celebrity*. New York: Routledge.

Lewis, C.S. (1991) *All My Road Before Me: The Diary of C.S. Lewis 1922–27*, edited by Walter Hooper; foreword by Owen Barfield. San Diego; London: Harcourt Brace Jovanovich.

Lewis, C.S. (2004) *Collected Letters, Vol. 2: Books, Broadcasts and War, 1931–1949*, edited by Walter Hooper. London: HarperCollins.

Lewis, C.S. (2014) *The Pilgrim's Regress*, edited and introduction by David C. Downing; illustrated by Michael Hague. Wade Annotated Edition. Grand Rapids, Michigan: William B. Eerdmans Publishing Company.

Lewis, Pericles (2007) *The Cambridge Introduction to Modernism*. Cambridge: Cambridge University Press.

Magnus, Margaret (1999) *The Gods of the Word: Archetypes in the Consonants*. Kirksville, MO: Truman State University Press.

Magnus, Margaret (2001) *What's in a Word? Studies in Phonosemantics*. Unpublished PhD Thesis: University of Trondheim.

Magnus, Margaret (2013) 'A History of Sound Symbolism', in Allan, Keith (ed.) *The Oxford Handbook of the History of Linguistics*. Oxford: Oxford University Press, pp. 191–208.

Milesi, L. (2008) 'Joyce's English', in Momma, H. and Matto, M. (eds.) *A Companion to the History of the English Language*. Oxford: Wiley Blackwell.

Molee, Elias (1890) *Pure Saxon English; or, Americans to the Front*. Chicago; New York: Rand, McNally & Co.

Molee, Elias (1902) *Tutonish: or, Anglo-German Union Tongue.* Chicago: Scroll Publishing Company.

Morgan, Thaïs E. (1995) 'Invitation to a Voyage in Cratylusland', in Genette, Gérard *Mimologics = Mimologiques: Voyage en Cratylie,* translated by Thaïs E. Morgan; with a foreword by Gerald Prince. Lincoln; London: University of Nebraska, pp. xxi–lxvi.

Morier, J. (1834) *Ayesha: The Maid of Kars* (1834). London: R. Bentley.

Noel, Ruth S. (1980) *The Languages of Middle-earth.* Boston: Houghton Mifflin Company.

Okrand, Mark (1985) *The Klingon Dictionary.* New York: Pocket Books.

Okrand, Mark (1997) *Star Trek: Klingon for the Galactic Traveller.* New York: Pocket Books.

Okrent, Arika (2009) *In the Land of Invented Languages: Esperanto Rock Stars, Klingon Poets, Loglan Lovers, and the Mad Dreamers who Tried to Build a Perfect Language.* New York: Spiegel & Grau.

Paget, Richard Arthur Surtees (1930a) *Human Speech: Some Observations, Experiments, and Conclusions as to the Nature, Origin, Purpose and Possible Improvement of Human Speech.* London: Kegan Paul & Co.

Paget, Richard Arthur Surtees (1930b) *Babel, or, the Past, Present, and Future of Human Speech.* London: Kegan Paul & Co.

Peterson, David J. (2014) *Living Language Dothraki: A Conversational Language Course based on the Hit Original HBO Series Game of Thrones.* New York: Random House.

Peterson, David J. (2015) *The Art of Language Invention: From Horse-Lords to Dark Elves, the Words Behind World-Building.* New York: Penguin Books.

Phelpstead, Carl (2014) 'Myth-making and Sub-creation', in Lee, Stuart D. (ed.) *A Companion to J.R.R. Tolkien.* Chichester: Wiley Blackwell, pp. 79–91.

Poe, Edgar A. (1838) *The Narrative of Arthur Gordon Pym of Nantucket*. London: Wiley and Putnam.

Pratchett, Terry (2010) *An Interview with Terry Pratchett*. Available at: http://www.amazon.com/gp/feature.html?ie=UTF8&docId=35534 (Accessed on 31 May 2015).

Prickett, Stephen (2005) *Victorian Fantasy*. Texas: Baylor University Press.

Ratcliff, John D. (2007) *The History of the Hobbit*. 2 volumes. London: HarperCollins.

Redin, Mats (1919) *Studies on Uncompounded Personal Names in Old English*. Uppsala: Berling.

Rosenfelder, Mark (2010) *The Language Construction Kit*. Chicago: Yonagu Books.

Salo, David (2004) *A Gateway to Sindarin*. Salt Lake City: University of Utah Press.

Sapir, Edward (1929) 'A Study in Phonetic Symbolism', *Journal of Experimental Psychology*, 12, pp. 225–39.

Scheunemann, Dietrich (2000) 'Cubist Painting, Automatic Writing and the Poetry of Gertrude Stein', in Scheunemann, Dietrich (ed.) *European Avant-Garde: New Perspectives*. Amsterdam; Atlanta, Ga.: Rodopi.

Schotter, Jesse (2010) 'Verbivocovisuals: James Joyce and the Problem of Babel', *James Joyce Quarterly*, 48: 1, pp. 89–109.

Scull, Christina (2000) 'The Development of Tolkien's *Legendarium*: Some Threads in the Tapestry of Middle-earth', in Flieger, Verlyn and Hostetter, Carl F. (eds.) *Tolkien's Legendarium: Essays on the History of Middle-earth*. Westport, CT: Greenwood Press. pp. 7–18.

Shaughnessy, Nicola (2007) *Gertrude Stein*. Tavistock, Devon: Northcote House.

Shaw Sailer, Susan (1999) 'Universalizing Languages: "Finnegans Wake" Meets Basic English', *James Joyce Quarterly*, 36:4, pp. 853–68.

Shippey, Tom (2000) *J.R.R. Tolkien: Author of the Century*. London: HarperCollins.

Shippey, Tom (2005) *The Road to Middle-earth: Revised and Expanded Edition*. London: HarperCollins.

Smith, Arden R. (2006) 'Tolkienian Gothic', in Hammond, Wayne G. and Scull, Christina (eds.) *The Lord of the Rings 1954–2004: Scholarship in Honor of Richard E. Blackwelder*. Milwaukee, Wisconsin: Marquette University Press, pp. 267–81.

Smith, Arden R. (2011) 'Confounding Babel: International Auxiliary Languages', in Adams, Michael (ed.) *From Elvish to Klingon: Exploring Invented Languages*. Oxford: Oxford University Press, pp. 17–48.

Smith, Arden R. (2014) 'Invented Languages and Writing Systems', in Lee, Stuart D. (ed.) *A Companion to J.R.R. Tolkien*. Chichester: Wiley Blackwell, pp. 202–14.

Smith, Arden R. and Wynne, Patrick (2000) 'Tolkien and Esperanto', *Seven: An Anglo-American Literary Review*, 17, pp. 27–46.

Smith, Ross (2007) *Inside Language: Linguistic and Aesthetic Theory in Tolkien*. Berne and Zurich: Walking Tree Publishers.

Solopova, Elizabeth (2014) 'Middle English', in Lee, Stuart D. (ed.) *A Companion to J.R.R. Tolkien*. Chichester: Wiley Blackwell, pp. 230–43.

Stein, Gertrude (1936) *Lectures in America*. New York: Random House.

Stein, Gertrude (1947) *Four in America*. New Haven: Yale University Press.

Stein, Gertrude (1966 [1933]), *The Autobiography of Alice B. Toklas*. London: Penguin.

Sweet, Henry (1897) *Student's Dictionary of Anglo-Saxon*. Oxford: Clarendon Press.

Sweet, Henry (1899) *The Practical Study of Languages*. London: J. M. Dent & Co.

Swift, Jonathan (2005 [1726]) *Gulliver's Travels*, edited with an introduction by Claude Rawson and notes by Ian Higgins. Oxford: Oxford University Press.

Thompson, Kristin (2007) *The Frodo Franchise: The Lord of the Rings and Modern Hollywood*. Berkeley: University of California Press.

Ulrich, Matthias (2002) *Esperanto: The New Latin for the Church and for Ecumenism*, translated from Esperanto by Mike Leon and Maire Mullarney. Antwerp: Flandra Esperanto-Ligo.

University of Reading (1972) *Supplement to the Calendar: Graduates 1928–72*. Reading: University of Reading.

Watt, Stephen (2011) '"Oirish" Inventions: James Joyce, Samuel Beckett, Paul Muldoon', in Adams, Michael (ed.) *From Elvish to Klingon: Exploring Invented Languages*. Oxford: Oxford University Press, pp. 161–84.

Wolf, Michael (2012) *Building Imaginary Worlds: The Theory and History of Subcreation*. London: Routledge.

Wright Joseph (1892) *A Primer of the Gothic Language: With Grammar, Notes, and Glossary*. Oxford: Clarendon Press.

Yaguello, Marina (1991) *Lunatic Lovers of Language: Imaginary Languages and their Inventors*, translated by Catherine Slater. London: Athlone Press.

Zweig, Stefan (1943) *The World of Yesterday: An Autobiography*. New York: Viking Press.